LIVING MEMORIES

A Memoir

Tim Smith
REAL ESTATE GROUP

Proudly Supports Moulton Museum &
'Living Memories: Nellie Gail's Memoir'

YOUR STORY STARTS AT HOME.

Scan to Watch our Viral 'Nellie Gail Lifestyle' Film

TIM SMITH
REALTOR | DRE#01346878

949.478.2295
tim@timsmithgroup.com
timsmithrealestategroup.com

COLDWELL BANKER
REALTY

F&M Bank is proud to sponsor the publication of this biography celebrating Nellie Gail Moulton, an artist, rancher, and community leader whose family legacy continues to shape Orange County. Like C.J. Walker, the founder of F&M Bank, Nellie and her family became pillars of the region, influencing their industries and development at the turn of the 20th century.

Both the Moulton and Walker families shared a strong commitment to hard work, innovation, and community, leaving an indelible mark on the area. This book honors Nellie's remarkable life and contributions, inspiring future generations to carry forward her legacy.

MEMBER FDIC

LIVING MEMORIES

A Memoir

NELLIE GAIL MOULTON
Edited by Scott T. Barnes

MOULTON MUSEUM PUBLISHING™

Living Memories
A Memoir

Nellie Gail Moulton

Edited by Scott T. Barnes

Published by Moulton Museum
Copyright © 2025 by Moulton Museum
All Rights Reserved
www.moultonmuseum.org

978-1-967781-00-3 ebook
978-1-967781-01-0 hardcover
978-1-967781-02-7 paperback
978-1-967781-03-4 audio

Cover copyright © Moulton Museum
Cover design by The Book Break team
Interior design by Allyson Longueira
Cover photograph by Eric Stoner

Contents

Foreword by Director Emeritus, The Irvine Museum

I am an art historian. In my seventy-eight years of life so far, I have earned a Master's Degree in Art History and, in my long career, have researched countless notable and significant figures on the history of California art. In 1992, I was the founding director of The Irvine Museum, a small but very active museum founded by Joan Irvine Smith and her mother Athalie Richardson Irvine Clarke. The Irvine Museum specialized in historic California Art, and I remained Director for twenty-six years until our institution merged with the University of California, Irvine.

In brief, after all the research I have carried out in libraries and books, after the numerous interviews I did with retired artists, widows, friends and children of artists, in my entire career, I have never been so present with an historical figure as when I read *Living Memories* by Nellie Gail Moulton.

As you read Mrs. Moulton's reminiscences, I assure you that you will indeed experience what I did upon engaging her narrative. You

too will not, in essence, be reading the text; it will be told to you in the most personal and gracious manner by Mrs. Moulton herself. You, as I was, will be chatting as two close friends do, about the amazing events of her long and remarkable life. The story you are about to read was written in March 1970, two years before she passed away.

Nellie Maud Gail Moulton was born on December 8, 1878, to John Lockwood Gail (1848–1926) and Prudence Adelia Stoneman Gail (1853–1894) in Irving, Kansas. In 1894, she traveled by horse and buggy to California to attend high school in the San Gabriel Valley. She then moved to Hebron, Nebraska, where she graduated high school valedictorian. As a young woman, she took a job in Seattle, Washington, to teach school. On a visit in 1903 to El Toro, California, to see her father who ran the general store and served as postmaster, she met rancher Lewis Fenno Moulton. They fell in love and a few years later were married in Camarillo, California, on November 29, 1908. That was the start of the amazing life and career which you are about to share with Mrs. Moulton.

Her life was difficult. In her day, Southern California was a semi-frontier, not at all like it is today, with a large, well-to-do population and every convenience one can imagine. No, in her day, nothing came easily and yet she managed to meet the various challenges she encountered on a daily basis. Her husband, Lewis Moulton, was a rancher, a profession that kept him occupied every day of the week. As a family, they had two daughters, which she effectively raised on her own. Sadly, Lewis passed away in 1938 at the age of eighty-three.

Once her family responsibilities were met and the daughters were grown, Mrs. Moulton started her long and notable career as an artist. She joined the Laguna Beach Art Association in the early 1930s and served as president in 1949. She was a popular member who organized and exhibited in numerous shows of this historic art group which in time became the Laguna Art Museum.

So, read this engaging memoir and share a pleasant, personal and informative experience with Nellie Gail Moulton, one of the founders of the Southern California we know today.

—Mr. Jean Stern
Director Emeritus
The Irvine Museum

Editor's Introduction

I last saw my great-grandmother Nellie Gail Moulton when she was 89 and I a lad of only four. She lived in a blue-and-white-trimmed home on what used to be Moulton Ranch on a hill overlooking the Pacific Ocean. Above the garage sat the all-important art studio. Inside, canvases awaited on easels, a palette of oil paints crouched in the corner, and Nellie donned one of her enormous hats to greet me and my family.

Fifty years later, I decided to see if I could find that home. With no map, no address, and without consulting anyone, I took to the road and drove directly to the home overlooking Three Arch Bay without any false turns. Mind you, I had never lived in this town or even this county growing up.

When I took my mom there on a remembrance trip, I confirmed the address. Yup, just as I remembered it.

Such was the kind of impression Nellie Gail had on people that a boy of only four, who had visited her home only once, could find it fifty years later.

I serve as treasurer for a beautiful little place called Moulton Museum which celebrates Moulton family and Orange County history, focusing primarily on the ranching period of the late 1800s to early 1900s. We also host an art gallery with revolving exhibits of international caliber.

Both of these legacies, the history and the art, sprang largely from the extraordinary woman whose pages you are about to read. A true pioneer, Nellie Gail traveled across the prairie in a covered wagon, grew up in a sod house, moved with her family from place to place as fortunes waxed and waned. Then, like so many ambitious young women, she became a schoolteacher and later a school principal in Washington state. Finally, from a chance visit to her father's general store, she experienced a romance worthy of Nora Ephron and a ranching saga worthy of Margaret Mitchell.

In later years, she participated in California's vibrant *en plein air* art movement, where the artist sets up her easel in the wild and paints like mad while the light stays true, usually completing a full canvas in under two hours. California is well-known for this because, well, the weather permits. Nellie studied this unique art form with such greats as Anna Hills, William Wendt and Edgar Payne, and has had solo exhibitions in places like SOKA University and Casa Romantica.

The descendants of Nellie Gail, myself included, feel that Moulton Museum represents Nellie Gail's story projected into the present.

People who visit often tell me that my family has an extraordinary history. My standard response is that everyone's family history is extraordinary. Every single person alive today has a history that includes famine and plenty; plague and healing; war, peace and backbreaking toil; the miracle of childbirth and the heartbreak of stillbirth; loneliness, heartache, and romance for the ages ... stories enough to fill a thousand novels.

All of us have extraordinary stories.

Every. Single. One of us.

The only difference, I add, is that my family wrote some of its history down.

However, it is true that if you examine carefully, some individuals experience fuller lives than others. As my fiction writing teachers would have it, "their stories take them to the limits of human existence."

Nellie Gail Moulton lived such a life.

What a privilege to edit my great-grandmother's memoir! Nellie began writing in Leisure World in 1968 and finished the manuscript two years later in her home in Three Arch Bay. Into the family collection it disappeared from sight and memory until, from the recesses of a musty closet, her grandchildren unearthed and donated it to Moulton Museum forty-nine years later.

I consider this project a major step in creating a memorable life of my own. I hope to live up to Nellie's legacy, her devotion to family and community, and her sense of honor. I did my best to preserve both word and style as closely to what she wrote as possible, with minimal editing. We have added footnotes for clarification, and longer endnotes to expound on certain topics of interest, in addition to including numerous photographs. Any errors in the notes or captions are entirely mine.

May you enjoy Nellie's story as much as I do.

—Scott T. Barnes
Editor, *Living Memories*

LIVING
MEMORIES

A Memoir

LULL'D IN THE COUNTLESS CHAMBERS
OF THE BRAIN, OUR THOUGHTS ARE LINKED
BY MANY A HIDDEN CHAIN. AWAKE BUT
ONE, AND LO, WHAT MYRIADS RISE! EACH
STAMPS ITS IMAGE AS THE OTHER FLIES.

—Pope[1]—

---

1. Often attributed to Alexander Pope, the quote originally comes from the poem "The Pleasures of Memory" by Samuel Rogers, 1792.

All of Me
PART I

❧

PIONEERS

*P*rovidence has widely bestowed upon us the noble gift of memory. As the years add up along this golden cord of life, thoughts of the past become a treasury of imagination, an endless image of faces, a voice long unheard, an affection that apparently came to an end and dropped out of life, only lying dormant—a note of music, a scent—even the stirring of a leaf will revive long forgotten feelings. They are, in truth, LIVING MEMORIES!

Now, at age eighty-eight, with 'my eyes needing all the help and my ears a tuning, too,' the heart will not rest in its urgency to summon, to reveal in some manner, the sad, the pleasing torrents of scenes, the rush of events. I dwell, ponder upon the fast and furious changes within the span of years since my birth, and the kaleidoscope becomes all the more incredible. My era has long vanished, it all seems like a dream, yet the vision of the many happenings is real, for I lived them, and IN THAT TIME.

Here, in these pages, if only in humble words, I want to leave something of my innermost self, tell you something of my yesterdays, and to particularly remember and know of the true Pioneer spirit that dominated your ancestors and how each, in his own way, helped to bring about, step by strange, miraculous, fantastic, preposterous step, the position our family holds today. And what is more amazing, to look out of my Laguna Hills apartment bedroom window, as I've done now for two years, and view this ambitious Cortese housing development called 'Leisure World,'[2] part and parcel of the land that used to be sheep country and here, properly, the Moulton Ranch.

Leisure? Indeed, it wasn't leisure in those virgin times. With each day a veritable challenge, much planning and labor, vicissitudes and hard living came before that. Lewis Fenno Moulton, an ambitious, adventurous, wide-eyed young man, just entering his twenties, set foot in California for the first time in 1874. My father, to settle permanently at El Toro, in 1903—this, the destined spot for Lewis and me to meet.

I was born a few days before Christmas, December 8th, 1878. Hardly an auspicious event or a gift to mankind—except to my loving parents, Prudence Adelia Stoneman and John Lockwood Gail of Irving, Kansas. I was the middle daughter, Alta, about five years older, and Katherine—Carrie as we called her—six-and-a-half years younger than I.

Nellie Maud Gail,
born December 8, 1878.

I was barely seven months old by the time a cyclone struck Irving. Mother was holding me in her arms, standing near the bolted window of one of the downstairs bedrooms when, suddenly, the terrific force and pressure of the rising storm forced loose the shutters, the wind, tearing through the room in its path of fury, shattering the pane and flinging mother, still holding me tightly, clear across the room and onto a bed.

2. In 1962, real estate developer Ross W. Cortese purchased the northernmost 2,775 acres of the Moulton Ranch for $6 million in order to develop the retirement community Leisure World Laguna Hills. (See endnote 1: Laguna Woods & Leisure World.)

Father was quickly at our side, and with Alta and mother's five-year-old little sister who was staying with us in tow, summoning all strength, slowly led us through inside doors; all the more difficult, for with the shaking and rush of great winds, they had slammed shut and tight and had to be pushed hard and with all might to pry open. Finally, reaching the doorway, father thought it prudent to hold back the two small girls, for the moment, in some hopefully protective niche; this of a necessity to more easily keep his clasp on mother and infant me as he first guided us to the outside, then quickly to struggle back to fetch the children. As he turned away from her to do this, mother began to hear alarming, crackling noises from the roof and top of the building, the very frame seeming to shudder against the howling winds. Fearing that debris would come tumbling down to crush them, mother frantically cried out in warning, all unheeded, for no human sound could come through against the angry show of nature. Providentially, all stayed intact and they came out to join us.

This was hardly accomplished when another fierce blast tore me from mother's arms, carrying me off near a pile of rocks. Lifting me up with lightning speed, father ushered us all around a corner of the building out of the worst of the winds. Cautioning us to hold tight, he then ventured to the barn to look at the animals and untie the horses.

With a lull, the winds seeming to subside, mother thought we ought to try to reach the neighboring frame house some distance away which could be seen still standing erect in the midst of the holocaust. Father, knowing full well the sudden, changing moods of these treacherous storms, wisely vetoed this suggestion, for when it was all over that very house was found crumbled to the ground, only the trembling, frightened horses were still helplessly tied to their roofless stall. Father quickly used his pocket knife to cut the ropes and free them.

At last, as the worst of the winds began to slow down, father undertook to re-enter the house to gather some blankets and bedding, and, thoroughly exhausted, the family stumbled off to the shelter of a plum thicket—there to stay the night.

Mother and father had worried that I'd been seriously injured at my fall but, with the light of dawn, the blood stains on my forehead and clothes proved to be that of poor mother's own cuts and bruises. Miraculously, none of us was badly hurt. Others were not so fortunate. Eighty-one people were killed in that community and town, a sad aftermath. That I survived this must have been part of God's plan.[3]

John and Prudence Gail, Nellie's parents.

Irving, Kansas, my birthplace, is no more. With water ever the precious commodity, it was abandoned years ago in order that it be utilized as a lake, where a dam was built across the Blue River, this to spill into the Kansas, on to reach St. Louis where the Missouri River joins the Mississippi, finally to drain into the Delta and out to the Gulf of Mexico.[4]

---

3. Some historians believe that L. Frank Baum named the protagonist of *The Wonderful World of Oz*, Dorothy Gale, after a girl of the same name who was killed by the two tornados that ripped through Irving, Kansas in 1879. In Baum's novel, a tornado sweeps Dorothy and her dog Toto from Kansas into Oz. (See endnote 2: Wizard of Oz.)

4. Founded in 1859 in the Blue River Valley, named after famed author Washington Irving, the city of Irving, Kansas, disappeared with the construction of

After that terrifying experience, father set his sights elsewhere. The opportunity presented itself to take up a government claim of 160 acres in Western Kansas, the terrain just short miles outside the town of Horace. To spare his family some of the initial hardships he went on ahead to prepare for our joining him. First, of course, there was the need for shelter. With the drive and ingenuity borne of necessity of those days, he proceeded to build a sod house on the land. This was the home we came to.

This land that father attempted to win over to his bidding was part of the open territory released as the result of the Kansas-Nebraska Act of 1854 (during the Presidential term of Franklin Pierce), enacted long before we came along.[5] The slavery controversy was then a bitter bone of contention, made doubly so with the proposals for a transcontinental railroad, following it with agitation to permit popular sovereignty therein. Settlers flowed in with disastrous consequences. John Brown, famous or infamous, according to what side you were on, in his fanaticism, operated an underground railroad to help slaves escape. This caused more trouble than help, both to the escapees and the citizenry. There were many brutal killings. It was a time of veritable local civil war; for all purposes, two opposing governments with elections called by one ignored by the other.[6]

Government land held the stipulation it had to be 'proved.' Proving meant just that—maximum production. Father tried his best. Within months, there was a fine watermelon patch, a sizeable cornfield, a young orchard planted, a healthy vegetable garden cultivated. But nature is both friend and foe and, first settlers up

---

the Tuttle Creek Lake, the second-largest reservoir in Kansas. (See endnote 3: Irving, Kansas.)

5. Passed during the lead-up to the American Civil War, the Act created the territories of Kansas and Nebraska. (See endnote 4: Kansas-Nebraska Act.)

6. A staunch abolitionist and proponent of armed resistance, John Brown led the infamous raid on Harpers Ferry. (See endnote 5: John Brown.)

to father's young manhood had their sole, challenging battle with mother earth. While the soil was new and had all promise of fertility, it needed every help to bring its treasures to fruition. The sun and rains blessed but, without warning, the dreaded winds and blizzards prevalent in that area came to bring havoc, or the droughts to scorch the newly planted corn and wheat seeds.

Even without the threat of weather conditions, there was the problem of marauding animals foraging for food, destroying crops. Prairie dogs, badgers and rattlesnakes abounded. Badgers were especially difficult to be rid of. As father poked his weapon into a badger hole, the animal dug furiously, faster than ever, first one hole then another to manage his escape. Father would finally get the little critter when he'd make the mistake of making the wrong turn scampering into an already dug hole.

Wild horses and buffalo roamed freely. For the buffalo, the dry land was especially hard. In their desperation for water, their resting grounds held depressions which had gradually formed by the weight of their bodies, useful as receptacles to retain water during rainfalls. The puddles would then increase the depth of the hole so that every drop was conserved. Even when the water was all absorbed there was enough dampness to help the poor animal.

Deer would come close to habitation. I remember on the farm, we children tried to catch a fawn amid the cornstalks. Apparently, the mother hid it too well, probably sending some kind of alarm to the baby to keep quiet so that, try as we would, we could not find it.

Another fun thing for us children was to climb to the roof of the barn to focus miles and miles away, right to where the men were working on the railroad, a sort of mirage.

Once, father, during a blizzard, almost got lost as he tried to wend his way home after leaving our relatives' house, only a short distance from us. Pelted and blinded by the fierce wind, sleet and snow, he misstepped his direction, literally going around in circles, until he finally bumped into a newly planted tree and then knew which way to go.

Indians would sometimes come to our door begging for food. These were dressed not in their native garb but rather, in spite of looking a little worse for wear, the same as other men, pathetic witness to their loss of identity.[7]

It was true and bare pioneering. A man had only himself—his indomitable will—his hands, brawn and heart. There were no mechanized implements to ease the burden. The words 'farm' and 'farming' did not have the connotation they have today. It was a way of life and a way of being self-sufficient. They had to be up to it—AND THEY WERE!

I don't think the homesteading venture lasted more than a year. No doubt, more than the risk, more than the harshness of weather conditions, the constant, never-ending vigil and exhaustive labor the undertaking demanded, father was ambitious and intelligent enough to be aware of a lost cause and so he gave it up and we moved to Horace[8] proper, where he set up a frame structure, designed in such a manner, to house a storefront and living quarters in the rear.

Mother accepted the move with great fortitude and grace, her deep Christian faith sustaining her in crisis. She cheerfully tackled and smoothed over, as best she knew how, the many discomforts that necessarily arise in setting up housekeeping in a new place. Consider how more so in a primitive atmosphere where all endeavor and all energy had to be summoned to reasonably

---

7. Kansas is named after a local tribe called the "Kaw Nation," also known as the "Kanza" or "Kansa" people. Today, four federally recognized tribes call the state of Kansas home. (See endnote 6: Native American Tribes of Kansas.)
8. The city of Horace was named after Horace Greeley, founder of the *New York Tribune* and a Republican nominee for president. (See endnote 7: Horace & Tribune.)

function. But there was the joyous element of love encircling us—mother and father never let each other stand alone—always, it was a family affair. This was the living, working creed of the pioneers, the undying spirit that built our nation. We were an infinitesimal part of it.

The Gail sisters in 1889, from left Nellie, Carrie and Alta.

In spite of this brave façade, it must have been an exhausting time for mother physically. A woman's work was literally never done. Cleaning was a burdensome task. Water for all needs had to be hauled to the kitchen in buckets from an improvised well, the drinking water spilled into a separate container or pail equipped with a ready ladle. When the range, which had to be fed and stoked continuously, was not crowded with simmering pots and pans—cooking included baking bread, putting up jams and jellies and preserves—the boiler would then take its stand on the stove filled with clothes that had had their vigorous scrubbing on a well-used washboard. Pressing time brought out the flatirons.

Other essential household chores that called for do-it-yourself know-how consisted of churning butter, salting meat, pickling, pouring candles and making soap out of grease and ashes, a tiresome, tiring and lengthy procedure.

As to apparel, while the all-encompassing utility general store stocked some items, even the traveling peddlers or service people bringing in occasional pieces of attire, among other wares on their rounds from town to town, clothing was, too, for the most part homemade. For mother, making a dress for herself or her girls was not merely a standard cover-up but accomplished with painstaking detail and consideration for style and what looked well. It was this creativeness in her that showed up strongly in her favorite hobby of hat making. Considering the extensive workmanship entailed in women's hats of those days, the finished product emerged almost as a work of art. Remembering this special gift of mother's, I can believe that she might have become a success as designer and milliner, even in those days of women's limited freedom, if time and circumstance had permitted it.

Not the least of worries for the pioneer mother, as with mine, was the occasion of illness. When it struck, the doctor, of course, would be summoned in great emergency, but with distance a problem and the danger of travel one had to depend on some innate knowledge or resort to home-made aids, or perhaps a particular patent medicine, if available. The usual family remedies for any number of complaints might include castor oil; springtime brought out sulfur and molasses; mustard plaster was generously applied for chest pains, eucalyptus oil for colds, etc. Housewives had to be practically quasi-physicians. I can still vividly picture the dear image of mother, her head bent in great concentration, pouring through her precious book, her own private medical advisor, referring to it constantly.[9]

While mother had her all-consuming role as wife and mother, father was surely head of his household. He was essentially a good-tempered man but at the same time, without displaying any undue harshness, made known his stand on family policy and discipline toward his children. I can remember 'most feelingly' that first and last spanking. I was fourteen and on this day had been acting up more

---

9. Home remedies have become in vogue in modern times—with mixed results. (See endnote 8: Home Remedies.)

than a bit willful, in fact, quite sassy to mother. Father, overhearing, quietly but firmly escorted me to the barn and paddled me. Most humiliating for one so grownup.

Our grandparents were much in evidence during our early growing up years. Grandfather Stoneman was a lay minister, a devout follower of Moody the evangelist,[10] a responsibility he took most earnestly. I recall him as a kindly and loveable old gentleman. One little-girl remembrance and joy is

John Gail with his wife Prudence (nee Stoneman) Gail, and her two sisters, Emma and Lida.

the times he and I went walking along the countryside picking ripe cherries. So was grandfather Gail a lay minister, but he not nearly so angelic as grandfather Stoneman. He was a man of little pretension, with a robust sense of humor. As a young man he'd thought seriously of entering politics, but though destiny led him toward a different road, he never lost interest. He gloried in campaigns and was absolutely in his element discussing the pros and cons of upcoming issues. He never could quite get the 'politician' out of his blood.

Grandfather Gail obviously instilled the venturesome spirit in father, as it proved in the years to come, but here I wish to note a memory of grandfather Gail as he relished telling the story of father's

---

10. Dwight L. Moody, 1837–1899, one of America's most influential evangelists, converted thousands to the Gospel in both Great Britain and America. He also invested heavily in the cause of abolitionism. (See endnote 9: Pastor Moody.)

running away from home as a youngster to join the Union Army. He, apparently, fibbed about his age, making himself older, but his father, nothing daunted, just as soon as he knew his whereabouts, journeyed directly to Camp Headquarters of General Ulysses S. Grant (this concession granted in cases of hardship or great emergency) to bring his youngest son back home and, at the same time, obtain the release of an older son stricken with typhoid fever. Father was not to be thwarted, however. He ran off once more, determined to join. This time grandfather threw up his hands. The fighting, though, in this Civil War of Rebellion was about at its end and father really didn't see much of it. About four years later, at a parade or march of the Civil War Veterans, led by General Grant, at a pause in their progress through town, spotting grandfather, [the General] actually remembered the past meeting and called him by name, taking time to exchange a few words.

Grandfather Gail was a first generation American, the family coming from England. There were ten children, seven boys and three girls. Two of the boys, grandfather's father and a brother, heard the call of adventure to the New World. They landed in western New York, around Buffalo, a point touching Niagara Falls, north, and the larger body of water, Lake Erie, southwest. Here they found work in one of the numerous lumber camps. With so many newcomers, the constant migration, the area a ready pathway to the rich valleys watered by the Ohio and other rivers flowing into it, the early settlers finding their spots of fertile land, lumber was needed to build cabins, churches, schools.

Great trees were felled, the logs driven by horse or oxen to the water's edge, rolled down a long chute to plunge and float with the stream to the sawmill. After the mill had done its work, the lumber would then be put onto freight trains to waiting rafts, tubs or boats, and on to its destination. To establish the period, this was the time when the notorious river gamblers were rampant. The loggers, catching the fever, did some betting on their own, but only as a moment's surcease from the heavy burden of their work. They'd try to guess toward which fork of the stream the logs would float.

Grandfather Gail, the 'erstwhile politician,' didn't set foot in a school until he was nineteen years of age but, like Lincoln, this didn't deter him from learning. The natural intelligence in him spurred him on to teach himself to read, write, do sums. He had a great sense of curiosity and imagination. Bible reading was a must. For anyone who could see and appreciate The Book, it had all the literature and all the human experience one could nurture and absorb. He did just that and coupled with his gregarious nature and talent for the spoken word, in no time at all, he had a teaching post and was chosen as lay reader for the Methodist Church.

Romance came to grandfather Gail soon after his start of teaching. That obvious charm won him a beauteous young bride, Alta Hamilton, one of his students. They became parents of ten children. I have no written proof, but it was said that Alta was a direct descendent of Alexander Hamilton, Secretary of the Treasury in President Washington's first administration, he who took so vivid a part in the beginnings of the American Republic as soldier, lawyer, writer, and appointed to the high position because of his valued aid to the General before his inauguration.

Mother's family also held ten children, seven girls and three boys. Her father, Reison Stoneman, first cousin to General George Stoneman of Civil War fame; her mother of Hathaway ancestry, the Hathaway name coming into prominence on more than one occasion. Mother was the oldest daughter. She was only forty when she died, March 30th, 1894, in Hebron. Another daughter, Mamie, married Simon Strader. Mamie left a two-year-old baby when she passed on and sister Lida helped care for the child. Later she married widower Strader. Sadie, still another sister of mother's, became Mrs. Bates. She tragically died in childbirth, complicated by an attack of scarlet fever. Sadie left two youngsters, Artie and Ray. Ray, just about my age, went through that same cyclone in Irving.

As a grown man, he became a banker in Eugene, Oregon.

It was grandfather Stoneman who took Sadie's little ones into his home. Everything he said and did proved the depth of his compassion and religious faith. He lived as he preached. In this atmosphere the youngsters thrived and were brought to respect the lasting values of life, the Bible and its teachings, the spiritual guide and solace. The boys were so learned in it they could recite almost every word of Matthew, Luke and John.

Mark Stoneman, Prudence's little brother and the photographer for most of these early family photos.

Other names I remember were Aunt Emma and Uncles Joseph and Mark. Mark was mother's youngest brother; he became a photographer of note. He had a way with children, particularly knew how to put them at ease so that, invariably, the picture showed up the 'very appealing child.' How proud we all were when Uncle Mark won first prize in a contest at a National Photographers' Convention.

Grandmother Stoneman died of lingering tuberculosis at fifty-four. After bearing ten children, she rested in 'time and space.' It was the first funeral I ever attended. Mother was born in Ohio, married in Iowa and died in Nebraska. The mention of these different locales bares the fact and harsh reality of the insecurity and the many hardships suffered in the necessity for moving, settling and resettling. In every sense, THEY WERE PIONEERS.

I was seven or eight when mother fell ill. She'd contracted some kind of typhoid or 'mountain fever' as they called it. The doctor came as often as he could and well I remember the times I used to run lickety-split down the road to the village pharmacy to have mother's prescription filled, my long blonde hair, in which mother took such pride, waving in the wind. During this very period the building of a stretch of the Union Pacific was going on. Jay Gould had arrived in town to look over his interests and could be seen daily getting on or off with his private physi-

Carrie (Katherine) Gail in 1886.

cian. On occasion, when he'd cross the road and pass our house the sight of Carrie and me playing in the sandpile would prompt him to pat our heads and tease baby Carrie into giggling.[11]

Mother was getting better but it would be a long time until she could be strong enough. It was thought best then that, to aid and speed her convalescence and recovery, she stay with her parents amidst the more tranquil surroundings of their fruit farm. And so she trained to Irving. Alta and I remained with father.

Horace was lost as far as father was concerned. In building the store and living quarters, as he had done, father started off with great hopes, fully expecting to do well, but in an underground kind of election maneuver involving the two competitive towns, Horace and Tribune, the final vote winnings surprisingly came to Tribune, even though it had

11. The general public reviled the Wall Street trader-turned-railroad tycoon Jay Gould, but those close to him told a different story. (See endnote 10: Jay Gould.)

a smaller population. It was something of a political scandal—sudden migration, as it were, bringing in people to the other side, quick additions to the in-residence voting rolls, even to stealing the town water pump in the middle of the night. This unethical procedure, nevertheless, won Tribune the County seat. Cleveland was president at this time, the Democrats holding the popularity vote. Too, the Depression[12] was on, people were prone to follow wherever there was hope of doing better. Later, Harrison won in a Republican coup.

For a lesser man than father all spirit would have been broken—without a doubt he must have been distraught beyond bearing—his wife ill, his home broken, the family stranded, in fact. And, the need now to establish himself in yet another place. But father had the will and resourcefulness, and so, first seeing mother off on the train and assured of her comfort, piled as much as he could of our belongings in the covered wagon, of a necessity abandoning the rest, the family cart securely tied in back, our old standbys and favorites, Coalie and Nig (so named by Alta and me) hitched and ready to go, off we started into the vastness and unknown of the still prairie land to cross Kansas.

Father had fixed a sleeping spot for us in the back of the wagon where we girls retired at each night's stop. Food and supplies and feed for the horses were purchased along the way at some general store. At each night's halt father would unhitch the horses, tie the long rope that would prevent their straying, then let them free to feed on the grass growth about them.

Our destination, of course, was to join mother in Irving, our trip in this manner so that mother would be spared the arduous journey, then on to Hebron, Nebraska, where father had kin, a sister and brother-in-law, also farmers. The plan was to find shelter at their home for just a while until he could explore any possibility to once again provide a sanctuary for his family.

---

12. Now called the Panic of 1893, this period represented the nation's most serious economic downturn until the Great Depression of 1929.

On the journey in the covered wagon along the rough, dry trails, we had an experience father handled very well, for it might have meant danger. Father began to notice two riders who seemed never to be too far behind us. There was no doubt they were following us. One night, at a stop, the horses unhitched, father at his watchful post, we girls, Alta and I, for all purposes, retired for the night, were awakened by some disturbance. Father, ever alert, hearing some rustling in the direction of the horses, whistled softly as was his wont in calling them to him. Alta and I peered from the wagon and heard father and the voices of the two men. Papa was 'telling a lie,' misinforming them as to what course we were traveling. We children were horrified! But, apparently, father had foiled the men from what suspiciously looked like a move to steal our horses, for when they trotted toward him at his whistle, one of the tethered ropes had already been cut. Father knew what he was doing—the remainder of the trip was accomplished without incident.

Losing the horses would have been a calamity, then and at any time. Lamentably, horses have been pushed on to practically oblivion by so-called progress in our civilization, but in those days they were the animals to prize, give consideration to, kindness and care. Sometimes a man was judged (there were, too, the brutal and insensitive ones) by the treatment he gave his horses and his control of them. They were our helpmeets, giving invaluable service in pulling, hauling, delivering. Coalie and Nig were our pets, as well. They were part of the family. They made such a good-looking pair harnessed to our fringed-on-top buggy!

Upon reaching Irving we found mother in good spirits and feeling better. After a short stay for visiting and getting mother and Carrie ready, again we took to traveling. Events following are a little vague, but it must have been that father put mother and we children on the train, he taking to the trails once more with the wagon and surrey and horses. Apparently, the family gathered together at some point along the way, for I remember a stopover somewhere near

Leavenworth, then known as a soldiers' drilling campsite. All about there was a strong sense of dissatisfaction and restlessness—a time of deep depression—for there was little work to be found. Harrison, the Republican, was in now, but soon they would want Cleveland again. The saying went, 'In God we trusted—in Kansas we busted.'

Hebron, Nebraska, our final stop and destination.[13] This was where father intended to take roots, permanently, it was hoped. We put up at Aunt Rhoda's farm until a rented place could be found for us. Here, father and a brother joined forces and established a building-contracting-carpentering business. Father located a suitable house and we moved into it. I can still picture it in my mind's eye and remember thinking it was the prettiest around. It had a sort of tiered layout.

The Hutchinson family where Nellie and family first stayed in Hebron, Nebraska: Uncle Frank and Aunt Rhoda (Gail) in foreground, their children Alva and Hattie behind.

First, the kitchen and dining area, steps to the living room or parlor, a master bedroom, a third lift had more bedrooms. The partnership prospered. Within three years, father was able to acquire a small parcel of land, three lots, on which he immediately tackled the building of a six-room house. It was at the rented house, though, that so much happened.

---

13. Founded in 1869 by "settlers belonging to the Disciples of Christ Church" in what was then Jefferson County, Hebron was named after the ancient city in the West Bank.

These were the struggling years and a time of sorrow. The Gails and the Stonemans were a close-knit family and so it was that they sought and helped each other in time of need. Mother, not too strong herself, ventured a train trip to Irving to fetch and bring home and care for her youngest sister, Libby, desperately ill with tuberculosis. She died a few months later at only eighteen years of age. And then, added grief with Aunt Emma and her baby. I came down with the mumps, then mother. It must have been a trying time for her, sapping so much of her energy and strength. There were so many things to attend to, to do all at once—the tension, the worry. Dear father and mother—they were indeed wonderful parents—never stinting their love for family and friends—helping when there was need.

Financially, however, the family's position had improved. As self-contractors now and having the know-how, father with the help of his brother built the six-room house mentioned. Father tried to make it everything a home should be. Aside from a comfortable interior, the front boasted a spacious lawn and flowers. There was a storm cellar, plenty of storing space for all perishables and preserves, the jars of berries and fruit, the barrels of apples, bins of Irish sweet potatoes. In the back, outside the porch, father dug a well and installed a pump device. Water could now easily be brought to the kitchen or toted to the barn for the animals.

Alta and I went to school. Carrie was still too young to attend. Characteristically, father and mother, while loving and patient, kept that disciplined hand. Alta, like mother, was strongly and artistically inclined, naturally creative. She excelled in music, took up painting. She was active in the church choir, had a fine soprano voice and was one of the first to sing solo. She met her future husband as a result of their mutual interest in music. I think he was a member of the same church but also quite in demand for the many get-togethers and socials, where he helped provide entertainment with his coronet. Alta, without a doubt, might have had a career, for she possessed all the requisites, looks, talent and presence, but her gifts were displayed in teaching for only a year and then love entered the scene. Alta became a bride at twenty. Here, though, I'm getting ahead of events.

Before the building of the home there was the time father decided to go speculating after that gold in Alaska he'd heard so much about. He and a brother-in-law started off with high hopes in their hearts— their dream to come back to their families laden with the glittering stuff they would

From left, Hattie, Alta, and Clarence, son of Uncle Harry in Chicago. Hattie was Aunt Rhoda's daughter; her maiden name was Hutchinson, not Gail.

find. Traveling by train as far as Seattle, they encountered such confusion and milling crowds, a veritable stampede of people, discomfiture, even the boats stalled, the rivers blocked in ice, that they were sharply brought to realize they could not possibly make the trek, as, too, the fact of having so little funds. They turned 'round to come back but, on the way to San Francisco, coming by way of the Strait, father became violently ill and seasick, and, as further ill luck would have it, while he was not aware and functioning, someone stole his money pouch and he had to wire home for money. And so our wanderlust father arrived home, bringing no gold, only himself. But that was enough treasure for all of us. We were all joyful to have him back, safe and sound.

There were fun times, too, during school days. There were holiday family picnics and parties, church socials. One I attended ended up in

*Band posing in Hebron, Nebraska, probably Arthur McHenry in front
holding the coronet, with Alta (Gail) behind his left shoulder holding the banjo.
Arthur and Alta married in 1893.*

an embarrassing moment. The young man I'd been paired with, sort of a school beau, was walking me home. We were engrossed in conversation, his hand touching my arm lightly, protectively, when suddenly, in an instant, the rapport was crushed beyond mending. We both toppled into a ditch. Charley White, the boy in question, became postmaster of Waterville, a town situated along the Columbia River in Washington. Years later, during my teaching period in Chelan, he came miles on horseback and sled to attend the housewarming party of mutual friends from Hebron who had migrated to and built a home on an almost inaccessible mountain slope in Washington.

Alta and I were proud of a new possession and certainly made use of it. We owned the second bicycle in town. It had really been sent out to Alta by our cousin, Clarence Gail, son of Uncle Harry of Chicago. When he had visited in Hebron some time before, he and

Alta had struck up a great friendship, almost close to being in love, I think, but, no doubt, the taboo on any romantic notions of first cousins nipped the thing between them in the budding state.

In midwinter there would always be the fun of sledding and ice-skating. Many a time, on weekends, when Uncle Mark, the photographer, came visiting, he and I took off to skate around the frozen waters, finally ending toward Aunt Rhoda's, then walk-ing the half mile or so up to the house. Usually we stayed overnight. Aunt Rhoda al-ways made us welcome.

The year 1893 was the hap-piest to remember as a com-plete family. We journeyed to Chicago for the World's Fair. Everything fell in smoothly. Mother was in better health, father content in his work, gratified that at last we were settled, permanently. And so father, mother, Carrie and I set out leaving Alta to re-main at home. Alta, joyously betrothed, with her heart's

Nellie in costume in 1892.

interest right there in Hebron, willingly stayed behind to caretake. There was the house and garden to watch over, the precious cow to tender and the care of the horses. We left Alta to these chores with the assurance that Uncle Mark would come out to help during our absence.

It had been arranged that we stay with Uncle Daniel during our stay in Chicago, a double pleasure. Uncle owned a good-sized home on Sangemon Street. There was a separate cottage on the grounds where we would be comfortably ensconced, our headquarters for the

*The Manufactures and Liberal Arts Building at the Chicago World's Fair, 1893
(a.k.a the Chicago World's Columbian Exposition).*

duration, although we would be visiting other relatives in the area as
well. Uncle Daniel had prospered as a manufacturer of bedsprings,
starting with a model patent. Eventually the business was sold out to
the Simmone group, this firm retaining Uncle's eldest son, John, in an
executive capacity.

The Fair of 1893 is set down in the annals of history as the first
large-scale venture with so many nations taking part in it and attempted in our country.[14] The international exposition marked the
400th anniversary of Cristoforo Colombo's discovery. In honor of
the courageous navigator the city was transformed into a veritable

14. Over 27 million people visited the Fair in 1893. Architects Frederick Law
Olmsted and Henry Codman designed the fairgrounds and 14 primary build-
ings on the shores of Lake Michigan, buildings which came to be known as the
"White City." Only the Palace of Fine Arts, now the Museum of Science and
Industry, remains. (See endnote 11: Chicago's World Fair.)

paradise of Renaissance buildings, the lake a shimmering lagoon, complete with serenading gondoliers.

The buildings, of course, housed the unusual, the treasures and artifacts of the representative countries. And, the fun rides. The great Ferris Wheel appeared for the first time, too, so named for George Washington Ferris who erected the structure. It rose 250 feet above the midway, carried a good number of cars, each holding many passengers. It was both thrilling and frightening rolling to the top, the winds from Lake Michigan whipping around you.

The Egyptian village was a popular attraction. The dancers, really corn-fed American girls, dark-eyed and dark-haired and obviously with very little training, performed their 'oriental dance'—simply a rhythmic posturing and swaying to musical accompaniment, using only the upper part of the body. The Fair had something for everyone—it was raucous, it was pomp and circumstance, parades, music, flowers, flags, fireworks. Mother and I were naturally and irresistibly drawn to the galleries. It was a particular thrill for me, for with schools taking part, one of my own 'works' was displayed at the children's center.

My 'escapade,' when that Gail sense of the venturesome took hold of me, is to be remembered. We had wandered to the manufacturers' exhibition building. Aware that father's minute examination of the machines was taking all his attention and mother not looking my way, I slipped out, dashing up the stairway to the roof and had a perfectly marvelous time running about and looking down from its heights. My absence discovered, father and mother decided to keep their post, thinking, and rightly so, that the errant wanderer would return to the point of leaving. When I finally appeared, I was scolded soundly, father even prompted to tweak my ear in his irritation and relief at finding me safe.

Chicago, coming up as the biggest metropolis, had begun many innovations. The elevated streetcars going along the Parkway down to Lake Michigan. An arena. I remember the horror we all felt when one of the stands collapsed during the 4th of July celebration in the days of the Fair. Many were seriously hurt. But the trip for us was a busy, happy time, visiting, sight-seeing. We came away exhilarated and with many memories of the stay.

Upon returning home, mother and Alta began to prepare for the forthcoming wedding. A seamstress was brought in to help with the trousseau. Unceasingly hands were busy, cutting material, ironing, sewing, sewing, until that last stitch was drawn. Alta's wedding gown, made of an off-white light wool weave, needed special, careful handling. My own dress for the occasion was of a beautiful changeable silk with full, pleated skirt.

Alta was married in a home ceremony with sixty guests attending. The new Mrs. McHenry was a lovely bride. Alta not only had the touch of beauty in face and form but even more important, her sweetness. She demonstrated this trait continually in so many ways. The editor of the *Hebron Journal*, a former senator, in printing her picture described her as one of the most beautiful girls in our town.

For their honeymoon, the couple immediately set out for Chicago and the

Wedding photo for Alta (Gail) and Arthur McHenry.

Fair. Alta, too, wanted to have a glimpse of all those wonderful things we'd seen, brought home to tell about. The newlyweds made it, arriving just the day before closing. Sadly, the trip proved an ill-fated one. Alta caught cold on the train and developed a cough and fever that would not leave her. She returned to her little rented cottage a very sick girl. It may have been that she tried to do too much while the family were away and, with the excitement and preparation for the coming nuptials, had run herself into a weakened condition. There had also been the discomfiture in rail traveling, for in those days it wasn't exactly a pleasant way to get to one's destination. Trains were run by coal, windows had to be kept open, the soot of the steam engine streaming into the coaches.

Now mother fell desperately ill. Mother, with all the changes in the past, the many uprootings, had somehow always tried to meet the situation, along with father, putting her shoulder against misfortune and pushing with all her might, never allowing a sense of despair to crush any member of the family. This was serious—it might have been a heart attack—she took to her bed, the town physician in constant attendance.

No doubt, even more than my still childish mind realized then, Alta, as the oldest, during these days, must have been thrown into great stress and strain. There was mother ill, her own health to worry about, and the thought of her imminent departure. Alta's health had worsened. Her lungs were now affected and the doctor strongly advised that she begin thinking of moving to a warmer climate—perhaps California.

A deep sadness enveloped the family. How many times would I come upon Alta weeping? The two, mother and daughter, had many talks, exchanged confidences. There was something prophetic in their behavior, as was, strangely, the similar vision they'd both had. Mother's was that she saw herself gliding along in a boat, clothed in flowing white robes and waving farewell to the family as she sped from shore. Suddenly, a beam of light fell around her and she saw the Christ. Alta did not disclose the fact of her own vision to mother, although she told me, in hers, at the beam of light, she had seen the Pearly Gates.

During these last days of her life, in speaking of her vision, mother suggested to Alta that she try to capture this apparition on canvas.

Dear sister, of course, assured her she would, and did, of a necessity using only crayons, which was not her preferred media, but she had been forbidden as a health precaution not to use paints.

Two weeks later, within a week of Easter, March 30th, 1894, mother passed away. I like to remember that she was at peace just before going to her great reward. As visitors came to her bedside, she wanted no tears, she'd ask them to sing and then listen, almost with a beatific smile on her face. She had known what the presentiment meant and it brought to her a sublime serenity. Only once did she express real sadness and regret. Out of Alta's hearing, she whispered, "Alta will not recover." Alta, at this very time, was so ill she could not attend the funeral. I was fifteen—old enough to feel the full impact of the loss. Mother was gone, forever!

Soon after, Alta and her husband left for California. They settled in a town called Covina, he finding work on a small orchard ranch, the grounds bearing grapes as well as the citrus fruits. Father, bereft and lost as he must have been at the tragic turn of events, worrying about Alta, after a while, decided it might be best for we two girls, Carrie and I, to join our sister in California, not only to be close to her but perhaps be of some help. And so, about early fall, we were put on the train, father greatly relieved with the happy circumstance of a young couple from Hebron who were traveling in the same direction and promised to keep a watchful eye on us.

I suppose it wouldn't have been me if we didn't go through the trip without a happening. This was the first time I had been entrusted to travel on my own with so many miles to cover and a little sister to look after as well. The train, going by way of Denver, of course, had the usual stops and junction turnovers. At one junction halt, I, busily engaged in talk in the next coach, suddenly became aware that there had been a disconnection and separation of cars, and ours was being pulled and moving in an opposite direction. Carrie was in there! With lightning movement I jumped off the train and ran to catch up to it. My fears were allayed when I was stopped in flight and assured that it was only to clear the area of the track, a procedure to either move or add other cars, I don't remember exactly which in this instance, but that Carrie's coach would be returned to the depot.

Arriving in Los Angeles, we were met by Alta's husband. As we jogged along the dirt roads our eyes grew big with interest and amazement at all we saw. Orchard after orchard, berries and fruits of all kinds, grape arbors bearing their luscious clusters in every size and color. This was the very season for every green thing to be ripe and in full blossom. We were thoroughly awed with all this beauty of nature.

Carrie and I were dispatched to school, already a month late in the term. The school building was typically country style—two rooms, two teachers, each tackling many grades. There was a man teacher for the upper, highschool studies, a woman for the lower. The school site was in a fork of three roads leading to and serving the towns of Covina, Azusa and Glendora. Youth adjusts quickly to change. It wasn't too hard to catch up with the rest of the class. I was pretty good at math, having a natural aptitude for figures, fair at algebra. Latin came a little harder.

Alta wasn't getting any better. While she was not bedridden, she had to do a lot of resting and be careful about not over-tiring. Oh, we helped after school, on weekends. There was the preparation for and putting up the preserves, a household must, getting the dinner ready, cleaning after, but it was Alta's husband who really tried with all his might. He was compassionate, unstinting in his care, carrying out all of the doctor's orders as best he knew how. He loved Alta dearly, wanted her well. The medical advice now was that it would be better for Alta to be in higher altitude and thereupon we moved to Glendora. Here, brother-in-law found placement at the LeFetre Ranch. Two brothers were in ownership, the family proving most kindly and considerate. The house we were to live in was on the grounds and fairly comfortable. It would have been a happy arrangement except that Alta was so ill. But the demands of life are inexorable—we continued as before—the difference, the distance to school a little longer. Sometimes I'd use Alta's husband's bicycle. Mostly, though, it was walking back home with the usual chattering and playful banter along the way with school chums.

Carrie and I made friends, some of these associations lasting a lifetime. How fate brings us all to a point of certain events with one move or another! Carrie and I came out to be with Alta but it turned out that, for the three of us, Carrie, father and myself, it was another step in the pattern of destiny. Carrie became a bona fide Californian, father met his second wife, the remarkable Minnie Raymond, and I, some time later, Mr. Lewis Fenno Moulton, over the counter at father's store in El Toro.

The simple act of going to school one morning almost ended in mishap. 'Sweet Marie Gordon' as we nicknamed her, Hope Washburn, another schoolmate, and myself drove out that day in Marie's horse-drawn buggy. Her father was a lawyer with offices in Los Angeles and the family well-known. We were going at an even trot when, somehow, the reins which Marie held between her knees in guiding the animal slipped out of her hands and laced around the horse's body, resting on the singleton. Marie quickly leaned over the dashboard to retrieve the reins but the sudden move frightened the poor animal, he swerved, kicked up his heels and broke into a runaway gallop. Marie safely fell on the soft earth at the side of the road and I, with more than alacrity, climbed on the seat, jumping out of harm's way, but Hope hit the ground hard and, I'm afraid, hurt her back. Horse and buggy out of vision, we struggled to our feet and slowly lumbered on to school. As we appeared within sight of the courtyard, an excited group of students raced toward us solicitously. When the horse had dutifully drawn up to the schoolyard, but the wagon sans passengers, they knew 'something was wrong.' We didn't miss classes that day, though, in spite of torn dresses and dirty faces.

Marie married a man high in political circles. Her brother went on to become the head of the Water Department in Glendora. They are still one of the first families of the city and instrumental in the start of the popular theatre movement in Los Angeles.

Father couldn't stay away from his girls and came down to see us the fall of our second year in California. I think he must have visited more than once for it was during this period that he met our stepmother—Mama Minnie—ninety-six now and still with zest for life.

Just before Thanksgiving, I found myself on the

John with his second wife, Minnie Raymond, "Mama Minnie."

train with father traveling back to Hebron. Carrie remained. This, after the assurance that Aunt Rhoda Hutchinson would come out to be with Alta and Carrie.

Father couldn't help but make the train trip fun for me and pleasant for those around him. Being naturally of a happy disposition, his quick wit and warm personality were infectious. Many of the passengers shared their baskets of food, turkey and trimmings, the stoves at the end of the car a popular get-together corner, not only for heating liquids but general camaraderie. Everyone tried to make it a sort of Thanksgiving celebration away from home.

Back to Hebron and to continue my high school studies. It was here I graduated. The year, 1896. It was also the year Alta passed away.

The traditional dress for graduation was, of course, white, mostly of cotton or organdie. We all wore white stockings and black patent leather shoes. My hair-do, as always, in two long braids. Later, as a young woman, I twirled these braids neatly up and around my head. It took hours to brush and put up. Hair was truly woman's crowning glory then.

My valedictorian essay was titled 'A Visit to the Coronado Hotel in San Diego, California.' During my stay with Alta, I had been taken on a long jaunt to that city and there to see the famed hotel. On this same outing it was for me, as well, my first glimpse of the ocean, traveling along the Long Beach coastline and on, all a memorable experience.

My dream and great desire upon graduating was to attend the University at Lincoln, but there were not enough funds and I hated to press Dad who had, in the meantime, remarried and assumed added responsibilities.

While I'd passed the examinations, had my diploma, giving me my license credentials, I was still too young to teach and so registered at the Seminary to gain an extra year of credits. After this I did teach, grade level, for about one year at the country school outside of Hebron. My mind, however, was so set on being able to enter the University that I followed through along another route. I registered for a business course at the Business College in Omaha. My plan was to make enough money to be able to go to the University eventually. There was a Fair going on in Omaha and I recall during the ride I took that 'new-fangled contraption,' the 'horseless carriage,' price, fifty cents for a drive around the grounds.

I hadn't quite finished my course when I received my 'very first telephone call.' It came from the proprietor of the largest store in Hebron asking me to take a position as clerk and bookkeeper, to start immediately. His former employee, a young woman, had unexpectedly quit to be married. I wouldn't have been John Gail's daughter if I'd refused. Here was an opportunity to use, and right-off, my business acumen.

I worked at the store for almost a year and then gave notice. It seems my good employer had ill luck in keeping his women employees. The reason was that I had received a teaching assignment call urging that I take the place of a beginning instructor who was having a discipline problem with her young charges. The challenge was too tempting. Starting my teaching duties, I became well aware of the general mood of disrespect in class. I made sure to put things right. With an especially insolent boy, one day I gave him the punishment he deserved, thrashed him in full view of the students. There was a minimum of trouble after that.

I taught in three country schools in the span of four years, from 1897 to 1902. Teaching became my career.

I was installed at the Roper School when father, ever looking for ways to improve his lot, hearing of a business opportunity, made the decision to move stock and barrel and take up a partnership in a store at Lake Chelan, Washington. Once more, a new place, a new home! His old friend, Judge Long, went with him on this trip.[15]

Father surely must have had great faith in this undertaking for he took all furnishings and belongings, including the horses and even the cow. Of course, I remained. Close to the end of the school term, father wrote to tell me of a teaching position open at Lake Chelan. Father was always looking out for his girl! This meant taking the Washington State examinations, which I was prepared to do. Since the examinations would not take place until the coming fall, I was inclined to give myself a vacation.

Nellie Gail Moulton
at nineteen years old.

15. Named after the Native Americans who lived in the area for thousands of years and called themselves the Tsillane, later spelled Chelan, which means "deep water" in their native language. Lake Chelan is the third-deepest naturally forming lake in the United States, only behind Lake Tahoe in California and Crater Lake in Oregon. ("Deep Waters: A tour of the people and places of Lake Chelan," National Park Service.)

The Chelan Hotel, built in 1901 by Caroline and C.C. Campbell.
Their son, Arthur, likely studied under Nellie Gail in elementary school.
Arthur graduated high school in 1907.

Training south on the Santa Fe, I stopped to visit with Vinnie Sperry, an old friend, who was now living with and keeping house for her brother, Roy, an engineer, stationed at the Gallup, New Mexico camp on a water drilling operation, putting down artesian wells for the railroad. Their actual living quarters was a box car, the crew occupying others. I lingered for three weeks. It was a most interesting and pleasurable stay.

Continuing on to Los Angeles, I visited with stepmother's people, old friends and, of course, Carrie. Vacation over, going by way of San Francisco, I trained north to arrive at Wenatchee and there to take the examinations. This, successfully accomplished, I boarded the boat going up the Columbia River to Lake Chelan, here to join father and to begin my new assignment. Arriving at the school, I was surprised and delighted to find that my good friend, Rose Long, was the principal. She was also teaching the high school grades. I was allocated to the grammar grades. This proved to be a most satisfying and enjoyable association.

At the end of the year, the school board was so pleased with our combined efforts that they tendered us a banquet, the affair held at the town hotel. The president of the school board also happened to own the hotel. I suppose this worked out very well expense-wise.

Long before this festive event, father had been forced to make still another change. It had sadly been revealed to him that all delinquent debts incurred in the past by his partner were being paid for with part of dad's stake. That necessarily left little in profit. He quickly and wisely decided to pull out, selling his share, simply noting it down as a bad bargain. With family affiliations now in California, he set out in that direction again. The more I dwell on father's sense of the right of things, his own fair dealings, his constant and cheerful spirit, the more I marvel at the strength of character he must have possessed to pertinaciously adhere through every circumstance of change.

The evening of the banquet that was given for Rose Long and myself proved to be a gay affair. A delicious dinner was served, dancing followed. I enjoyed every minute of it and I think I danced almost every dance. One particular gentleman, who, I learned later was a traveling representative of a business firm in Seattle, and at

Five teachers in the state of Washington; Nellie is second from left.

the moment a guest of the hotel and invited to join the party, sought me out frequently as a dancing partner. ('You see, my dears, I want you to know that this ancestor of yours was no wallflower.') He was handsome, debonair, had a good sense of humor, danced well, and, obviously, was quite a conversationalist. We rather hit it off and he later courteously walked me home to my lodgings.

Well—that was the extent of our acquaintance at the time, but he comes into the picture later in a very funny incident.

And now the Christmas Holidays came along. Rose Long, Myrtle Benson and I set out for the State Teachers' Convention scheduled to take place in Seattle. We took the Columbia River boat to Wenatchee, there to board the great northern train to Seattle. We were told that the trains had just started to roll through for the first time in five days because of the severe winter slides, the heavy snows piling along the trail. There were no sleepers as it was just a few hours run. It was also the only through train to Seattle. We had scarcely reached a mountain town when there were some new slides and, of a necessity, a long wait to clear the tracks. The town was covered with deep snow and crusted ice. It was too tiresome and uncomfortable to sit and wait inside, and so most of us got out to do some sightseeing. We joined some of the townsfolk in sled-riding and snowball throwing. One young gentleman passenger, sympathizing with the three stranded young ladies, at our return to the coach, invited us to join him in the dining car. After our repast, we started a card game that lasted through most of the rest of the ride. We had turned over one coach seat to face the other so that we could do this. At one point, one of the brakemen, coming through the aisle, whispered to us that after our train had passed the temporary bridge the jar had precipitated yet another slide behind us. Fortunately, we were free of it. The rest of the journey went smoothly.

The gentleman-in-question turned out to be a 'Mr. O. K.' (Those were his true initials and I prefer to identify him this way.) He was on the staff of the Seattle newspaper, the *Post-Intelligencer*. He rather favored me particularly and I saw him again after that. We corresponded. He took me to dinner now and then; we saw plays together. He kept track of me. It was fun to be with him. No romance. He teased me about the coincidence of our initials. 'He was O. K. while I was N. G.'—and 'Was there ever a chance of my becoming O. K.?'—and 'At least there was no danger of his becoming N. G.'[16] An enjoyable friendship, harmless flirtation.

Vacation at hand, I prepared to leave for California, for I wanted to see my folks. I wasted no time. With visions of having a pleasant two days in town before boarding the boat that would take me down the Pacific coastline, I entrained that first Friday evening of the weekend to arrive in Seattle close to midnight. I remember the gallant gentleman at the depot who carried my bags on the short walk to the hotel. Tired and ready to put my head on a pillow, the clerk announced that there were no rooms to be had. The city was milling with people, coming in at all hours, in order to greet the President, Theodore Roosevelt, who was expected to go through the next day. It was suggested I try the smaller hotel across the street. This was somewhat annoying, but little did I suspect it was only the beginning of a weekend that would turn out to be a sort of 'Comedy of Errors.'

The next morning, I left a message for Mr. O. K. at his office, advising him of my whereabouts. We had previously planned an outing and, of course, I wanted to let him know where to reach me. When he called the hotel, somehow, the operator mixed the wires and we could not connect, even though I was in my room all the time. On my part, naturally, I was puzzled at receiving no return call, but when I finally came downstairs to find O. K.'s note, I knew what had happened.

Upon meeting, O. K. reluctantly blurted out something unexpected had arisen that required his immediate presence in Tacoma. We would rejoin, he said, later in the evening. So that we could spend

---

16. N.G. was used as an acronym for "no good."

the interim together, he suggested I ferry with him, have lunch on the boat, he to get off at Tacoma and I to remain aboard, returning to Seattle as it made its circle around the Puget Sound. Alighting at Seattle and walking back to my hotel, I passed two men talking. One was the very same gentleman who had danced with me at the banquet in Chelan. He turned, recognized me and, apparently his conversation over, came toward me in greeting. We chatted a bit, and then he made the request of a date to get reacquainted. I knew my meeting Mr. O. K. would be quite late, and so I consented to, at least, ride along the lake edge with him on the scenic trolley. It would do no harm and I'd be back in plenty of time. So I thought!

I went immediately to my room to freshen up and rest, the arrangement being I meet him after a while for the trolley trip. But, as circumstance would have it, just as I was about to start off, there was O. K. on the phone announcing his return and much sooner than I'd counted on. Now, here was a dilemma! What else could I do but confess. I told him of my commitment and how it had come about. Seeing the humor of it, he laughed, and said, of course to keep it, he'd stay right there waiting for me. And so I went on, but, as fate would have it (the plot thickens), at the end of the line and the point where the trolley is pullied to make its return trip, it missed the connection, jumped the tracks, and all passengers had to get out until it could be realigned. Now, here I was in another fix! O. K. might be thinking the worst! Once more I had to plead guilty. I revealed the fact I was worried about being late as I had a friend waiting. He advised telephoning. O. K. understood but 'just to make sure' he planted himself at a viewing vantage point at the larger hotel across the street so that he could see me getting off that first trolley. When we finally arrived and O. K. walked toward us, the two men shook hands amicably. O. K. teased me more than ever after this incident. "So this, indeed, was the small town girl!" he chided, playfully.

The next day I took the steamer sailing to San Francisco, there the train to Los Angeles and on to El Toro where father now ran

El Toro General Store and post office with a mystery woman posing on the near side of the railroad tracks, reprinted, with permission, from the historical collection of First American Financial Corporation. All rights reserved.

a general store and post office.[17] It was on this trip I met the lady who was a close friend of Mrs. Randolph Hearst, the publisher's wife. We'd become friendly on the boat. When we disembarked at San Francisco she asked whether I'd like to meet Mrs. Hearst. We drove downtown to the Hearst Building where Mrs. Hearst occupied a tower apartment. We were both disappointed to find she was out of town, I more than she for I missed knowing that fine lady.

---

17. John Gail and daughter Carrie ran the store for about two years, approximately 1901–1903. The name of the town, El Toro (The Bull), came from the Native American ranch helpers who began to refer to the land as El Toro due to the herds of cattle headed by "bellowing bulls." (See endnote 12: El Toro & El Toro Store.)

My next stop, El Toro. With father's confining hours tending the store, I spent considerable time around the place and sort of helping out. One day a Mr. Moulton, one of the ranchers, came in to get his mail and make a few purchases. Father introduced me and I helped wait on him. We exchanged some pleasantries, then, his errands done, he left. Nothing more. My only and immediate impression was that he seemed a very nice gentleman of a customer. That was the summer of 1903. Five years later I became Mrs. Moulton.

California at this period didn't interest me in the least, neither the climate nor the terrain. I remember father taking me on a sightseeing tour along the ranch sites, down the Laguna dirt roads, the beach coastline and up Aliso. It all looked like wasteland as far as I was concerned. My life would be spent 'far and away' from any such place. I could only remark, "I wouldn't live here if they gave it to me!"

I didn't return that next year. While at El Toro, I'd received a wire calling me to fill a vacancy at Port Orchard, Washington, where there was an overflow of students. Arriving at the school, I was pleasantly surprised to find two friends and colleagues, Marie (Gordon) and Maude, both having taught at the old Thayer County school outside of Hebron.

Marie and I rented a suite of rooms from a lady with two children who ran a small establishment. Her husband taught school in Nome, Alaska. She was an accomplished musician and painter and conducted a studio on the premises. It was really at this time in my life that I began to be deeply interested in the art of painting, taking lessons from her. She was even a student of the occult, conducting occasional seances; a versatile and interesting individual.

My first efforts on the canvas were not exactly outstanding. I can still hear the comment of a gentleman student of our landlady. I had painted an outdoor scene, trees around the edge of water. I placed a large rock somewhere in between. I viewed it critically. 'Not so bad,' I mused. I asked the man what he thought of it. Pointing to the 'rock,' he replied, "That's a pretty good-looking potato."

But Nellie Gail wasn't to be downed. There I was, daubing at every opportunity, though, I must confess, the opportunities, or rather the dedicated inclination came seldom. This was the year of enjoyment as well as hard work. Bremerton, the Navy Yard, was across the Bay from Port Orchard. On certain weekends, with government sanction and approval, the anchored boats were used by the officers for dance affairs, we teachers especially marked for invitations. A launch would be sent out to pick us up, then bring us back safely to shore and home after the festivities. I was about twenty-three then, with all youthful energy, able to dance the whole night

The oldest Nellie Gail painting in the Moulton Museum collection and quite different from her later style.

A typical Nellie Gail seascape.

through and be fit and alert for the next day's work.

O. K. used to come out to see me. One Sunday we rented a rowboat and put out to one of the islands, tied the boat, and wandered around, as did others. We talked and walked and laughed, probably acting silly, cut our initials on a tree, generally having a good time. Of a sudden, we became aware that it was kind of getting late and the place looking deserted. We rushed back to our boat only to find it gone. The tide coming in had loosened its moorings and pulled it away from shore. We could see it out there at a distance. Both having healthy lungs, we put them to use and started 'hallooing' as loud as we could, hoping we'd be heard. With sound carrying so well on water, one of the regular crew cruising boats from the marine base soon heard our call of distress, quickly took in the scene, rowed to our disappearing canoe and floated it back to us.

After Port Orchard, I was elected and assigned to a principal-ship at the Dunlap School, situated in the suburbs of Seattle, along Lake Washington. There were seven buildings, all part of the Seattle school system and all under one superintendent. I was principal of one. It was a busy, active period.

One Friday, at recess, one of the little girls ran up to me with the mail to hand me a special message. It was from Mr. Moulton. This was the first actual and direct correspondence I had ever received from him. Father had mentioned him once or twice in his letters and he had sent on books and baskets of oranges shared, and a treat to those of us living in the north country. That was the extent of any contact. The message had been sent from Kentucky. It stated he would be arriving in Seattle at eight that evening, for me to meet the train and be his guest for the weekend.

When I left El Toro to return to Washington, he joined the fam-ily to see me off at the depot, casually mentioning he would be going to Boston on business that winter and would possibly return by way of Seattle to see me. This was the visit.

With little time for preparation, I took the evening boat to Seattle, meeting the train on time. We taxied to the hotel, settled our individual room arrangements, then, over a late supper, made plans for the fol-lowing day. I told him my desire was to see *Ben Hur*, the much-talked-about play, currently showing to capacity audiences in the city.[18]

The next morning, meeting for brunch, Lewis regretted he had not been able to obtain the tickets as yet, but that he would make it his business to. With complete sellout at each performance, even O. K., with his newspaper contacts hadn't been able to wrangle two more tickets.

18, Penned by a Civil War general, *Ben-Hur: A Tale of the Christ* became one of the most impactful stories of all time. (See endnote 13: *Ben-Hur*.)

Once more, Lewis set out to try his luck, and succeeded. That evening, Lewis put himself out to make it an enjoyable one for me—dinner at Rathskeller's and then, the pièce de résistance—the surprise—at the theatre we were ushered to box seats. The play met every expectation, magnificent and colorful. In those days, background scenery, although done with great skill, was hard to set up to give utmost in reality, the treadmill visible to the audience, worked by the backstage crew. Live horses were harnessed to the chariots. A marvel and great effort for that time. As the curtain went down on the last act, it took a while to come back to earth and the mundane present.

The next day, Sunday, after lunch, Lewis escorted me to the boat landing. We said our goodbyes. I went back to my teaching; he returned to his ranch.

Apparently, as the future revealed, he had other things in mind, but I must honestly say that seeing him to me was simply a touch of friendship and nothing more than having the attention of a very nice gentleman, and what girl doesn't enjoy that!

With the coming of summer and vacation at hand, again I was drawn to thoughts of family. Father had gone from El Toro and was living in a town called Monita, somewhere near the beach, not far from Redondo. It was wonderful to be close to loved ones, so much so that when fall drew near and my return to Washington was imminent, I made a decision. I sent in my resignation to the Seattle Board of Education. It was the year 1905.

With the certainty of my remaining in California, Carrie and I talked of the possibility of having an apartment of our own, she to continue her music in earnest and I to ferret out a business position. After all, I had my skill of shorthand, typing and bookkeeping, and, counting that store in Hebron, even some experience. In following this goal, I registered for a refresher course, eventually locating with a wholesale firm in the heart of Los Angeles, then the center of business activity. Our plan to take up housekeeping together didn't materialize—Carrie became Mrs. Drews before we could get to it.[19] I continued working and for a while, my daily routine was boarding the trolley to Los Angeles each morning and then going back to Monita.

Carrie with her husband, Fred Drews. The two married September 21, 1907, in Santa Barbara, California.

An occurrence along this time had me in the clouds. I was certain my fate and future had been sealed. Stepmother's younger sister was taking singing lessons from the choirmaster of our Methodist church. He also maintained a private studio. One day I accompanied her. After the session, the professor suggested I test my voice. As I ran the scales and sang a song, he seemed pleased. 'You have a fine contralto,' he enthused, 'and a magnificent range up to F; there were great possibilities.' 'So much so,' he went on to say, he would give me free singing lessons up to two years, and, 'perform under his management.' It was all settled!

19. Carrie Gail Drews, Nellie's sister, married Frederick George Drews and had three children: Rudolph (killed in a hunting accident as a Tustin High School senior), William L. Drews, and Prudence. Fred farmed a 1,000-acre lease on the Moulton Ranch, raising barley and black-eyed peas. Later, he gave up farming and took over management of the Moulton Warehouse in El Toro. When they sold the warehouse, he was put in charge of maintenance on the Ranch until his retirement in 1950.

I came away feeling like an accomplished diva. I could almost hear the 'encores' of the admiring audience. But life can lift you up to the stars or down on your knees. I 'never' did have that first lesson. The maestro's father suddenly passed away in Canada and he had to leave to attend the funeral and settle the estate. He stayed. And so my operatic career ended even before it began.

I was seeing Mr. Moulton frequently. His ranch holdings were, of course, some distance from Los Angeles, but with most of his business transactions and banking consummated in town, for convenience sake, he had long rented a suite of rooms in one of the family hotels then abundant along the Plaza. Often he traveled to the city and invariably came out to visit the family, and me, particularly. We went to concerts, the theatre, out to dinner. He acquired a new Buick, a single-cylinder affair, one of the first in automobiles of its kind. It was fun to learn to drive it. He'd leave it for me to use while he was away. A drive to the countryside was enjoyable—no traffic menace. We'd go to the beach at Santa Monica—Venice was a gay, popular spot then. Watching the boats come in at the San Pedro Pier was another pleasurable pastime.

Father's family was increasing. I had little brothers to love. With time, I had arrived at a pattern of living and thinking. My friendship with Mr. Moulton was blossoming into more serious aspects. It was becoming more and more apparent in his persistent attentions.

All of Me

PART II

LEWIS FENNO MOULTON

*L*ewis Fenno Moulton was born January 17th, 1854, his father Master-in-Chancery of the Chicago Courts and a well-known attorney. His clients included many important people, one in particular, Marshall Field.[20] He also had some interest in and took part in the beginnings of the Chicago Tribune.

Lewis' mother was Charlotte Fenno, of the socialite Fennos of Boston, Massachusetts. Lewis had a brother, three years his junior. He was told that at one time Abraham Lincoln bounced him on his knee. Since Lincoln was also an attorney and, at the time of Lewis' infancy, a member of the Illinois State Legislature, in all probability this very incident did take place at some family social function or other, for there was a good deal of calling at one another's homes.

The boy was still in grade school when his secure world of family life suffered great upheaval in the loss of his father.[21] Charlotte

---

20. Begun in 1854 as P. Palmer and Co. in Chicago, made famous by its "satisfaction guaranteed" return policy, the Marshall Field and Company department store chain grew to 150 stores by the turn of the century. Its storied history continues through its present-day incorporation into Macy's (Twyman, Robert W., *History of Marshall Field and Co.*, 1954).

21. Lewis' parents, Jotham T. Moulton and Charlotte H. Fenno, divorced in 1864 when Lewis was 10 years old. His father stayed in Chicago, while Lewis went with his mother to Boston to live close to her family (Moulton Museum archives).

Fenno, a lady brought up in the strictest sense of tradition, sheltered from childhood, without a doubt, at this time in her life, experienced great unhappiness and bewilderment. Worse to follow was that the money in trust allocated to mother and sons, within a short period, dwindled considerably. The details are not known to me, but being unaccustomed to the maneuverings of the financial world, she may have accepted some ill advice as to investments. The only route to follow, under the circumstances, was to return to Boston, in this way having the comfort of being close to her family and the assurance of her brother's protection and guardianship. Mr. Fenno was one of the largest export wool merchants trading out of Boston, doing business in as faraway places as South America, Australia and New Zealand, as well as in the States.

Portrait of Irving (left) and Lewis Fenno Moulton. In 1864, ten-year-old Lewis and seven-year-old Irving moved with their mother Charlotte to Boston.

Settled in their new surroundings, Lewis, still a young boy, together with his brother, continued his schooling. Boston was then considered 'the most proper city,' even provincial and one hundred percent Republican. But perhaps the social historians were not quite correct, for the 'independents,' too, were most voluble and, as to being stuffy, the following ditties used in later years in advertising brought smiles as well as customers.

The Fenno Family home in Boston.

One was:

"Famous Flexible Finish
Collars Cannot Crack"

Another:

"Pedal Integuments
Artistically Illuminated
For the Infinitesimal Remuneration of
5¢ per Operation"

The years quickly rolled by. The boy now growing into manhood, as the eldest, began to show his stature by insisting on earning his keep. Encouraged and helped by his merchant uncle, he began an apprenticeship at the Daniel Webster Farm, located outside the city and near the sea. His wages—$100 a year and found. The farm's operations consisted of gathering kelp, grinding and pulping it for soil and fertilizer use. Naturally, other duties must have included hoeing and planting, care of the animals, etc. This first taste of farming and ranching experience directly sealed his destiny, colored the events of the rest of his life.

Lewis had a goal and it was that when he had enough saved he intended to go West to seek his fortune. He never swerved from this ambition. Even in youth, he was serious and methodical, a trait that stood him well in the years to come as he fell upon opportunities and proved equal to challenge.

He was barely in his twenties when he started out—not with a knapsack on his back, but with an important piece of paper, a letter of introduction from his Uncle Fenno to Mr. James Irvine, Sr., of the vast Irvine Ranch in California, the ranch, part of the old Spanish land grants, and one of Mr. Fenno's wool-dealing posts. With the blessing of his mother, he boarded a boat sailing down to the Isthmus of Panama, then by rail to cross to the Pacific coastline, there to take a steamer, one of those barely out of the windjammer stage, to the port of San Francisco—south on another and smaller boat to finally arrive at Anaheim Landing, near the now city of Los Angeles. This in 1874, the country still in turmoil following the War of the Rebellion.

The next move was to hire a rig, and so to make his first night's stop in the sleepy village of Santa Ana. In the morning he set out for his final destination, the Irvine Ranch. Arriving, he presented his letter to Mr. James Irvine, who immediately took a liking to the boy and handed him into the care of his good manager, a Mr. French.[22] Here, too, there was instant rapport. He was hired on the spot at $35 a month and keep. Quite a promotion!

---

22. Charles E. French visited warm, dry Southern California with the Bixbys from Boston for health reasons. The owner of Rancho San Juaquin, James Irvine, Sr. convinced French to become the ranch's first manager. In a letter to his wife, French described the rancho as, "a God-forsaken land with coyotes barking, wild cats screaming, and not a light to be seen anywhere in the darkness of the night" (Irving Ranch History, "From Mexican Land Grant to Great Irvine Ranch"). Eventually, Moulton and French leased a swath of land from Oceanside to Wilmington to raise sheep. Moulton later bought French out (Whitcomb, Janet, "A Ranch That Stood Where Malls Now Reign," Patch, 2012).

James Irvine, Sr. had come to the new world from Ireland. He, too, along with many of the immigrants debarking at the port of New York, found work at the paper mills. In 1849, he joined the stampede to California, on the boat to San Francisco making a chance acquaintance that started a long sequence of events, eventually leading to the creation of the Irvine Ranch. By the time Lewis came on the scene, the Irvine Ranch had become a large and profitable sheep and sheep-grazing proposition. Indians were invariably employed for the shearing, the wool shipped from Newport Bay to San Francisco and there transhipped to wool merchants in New York or Boston. This was the connection between Rancher Irvine and Merchant Fenno.[23]

Areas of southern California, not far from the coast, with its streams of water flowing through the valleys, providing its own means

23. The Irvines, who immigrated from Ireland during the Potato Famine, purchased Rancho San Juaquin from distressed ranchers during one of California's many droughts. (See endnote 14: James Irvine Sr. & family.)

of irrigation and fertile soil, were resplendent with the blooming of grape vines and orchards, but the part Lewis came to know best was sheep country, down from San Diego to Los Angeles. The young man also found himself designated as chore boy. He ran errands, drove the children to school at Tustin and generally helped around the ranch—all this marked down as valuable experience.

Lewis was presented with one chore he hadn't counted on. The day arrived when Mr. French asked him to quickly fetch the horse and buggy and rush the expectant Mrs. French to the hospital, all the way to Anaheim. That baby became Mrs. Burns and, by then, the French name was important in banking circles.

The young newcomer was capable, untiring in his efforts. He did so well, in fact, and his association with Mr. French was so amiable and rewarding, that the older man suggested they go into a partnership. Mr. Irvine was now leasing and renting land areas for grazing. There was money to be had in sheep running. Lewis wrote to his uncle to tell him of this opportunity, asking for a loan.[24] Fenno, aware and knowing exactly what it would mean, sent his nephew nineteen-hundred dollars—precisely the amount he had spent on Lewis' younger brother for his education, together with the happy stipulation that it was not to be returned. With this capital, resources combined, he and Mr. French procured their sheep and went into business.

The first year for Lewis was such a profitable one he was encouraged to take yet another step. Apparently, with Mr. French amenable to the idea or, perhaps, offering to do so, he bought out Mr. French. Now he was on his own—Rancher Moulton—even to trading with Uncle Fenno. He had learned his way, knew every facet of ranching, and was known and respected not only for his business sense but his fairness and honesty in his dealings with others.

---

24. Lewis' maternal uncle John B. Fenno, 1817–1894, who apparently had spent $1,900 on younger brother Irving's education.

Form No. 168.

THE WESTERN UNION TELEGRAPH COMPANY,
INCORPORATED
23,000 OFFICES IN AMERICA.   CABLE SERVICE TO ALL THE WORLD.

This Company TRANSMITS and DELIVERS messages only on conditions limiting its liability, which have been assented to by the sender of the following message.
Errors can be guarded against only by repeating a message back to the sending station for comparison, and the Company will not hold itself liable for errors or delays
in transmission or delivery of Unrepeated Messages, beyond the amount of tolls paid thereon, nor in any case where the claim is not presented in writing within sixty days
after the message is filed with the Company for transmission.
This is an UNREPEATED MESSAGE, and is delivered by request of the sender, under the conditions named above.
ROBERT C. CLOWRY, President and General Manager.

RECEIVED at LOS ANGELES, Cal.

503sf qm m 17 collect   244

He Boston,Mass.?july 22-04

Lewis F.Moulton,

      Los Angeles.

Spring wool sold twelve half market stronger now advise shipping

lambs if good condition otherwise sell.

                    L.C.Fenno

                    11:18 a.m.

Telegraph dated 1904 between Lewis Moulton and Lawrence Fenno.

His friend, Kaspare Cohn, 'head' of the Union Bank, knew it well. Kaspare had come into this country as a Jewish immigrant. With the help of and getting together with a group of his own people, a loan bank was started, these loans mostly directed to ranchers, the sheep men, for they needed money to add to their flock, to pay the herders and shearing men. The bank began with one room in a building near the Plaza in Los Angeles, employed one teller, one bookkeeper. Next, they rented a floor above some stores on Broadway, and finally built their own headquarters at 8th and Hill Streets. Today, the Union Bank has branches nationally and is growing all the time. The point is that Lewis and Kaspare became friends, not merely business associates. There was always a place set for Sunday dinner at the Cohen home, whether Lewis could make it or not. Cohen would tell Lewis, "Take what you need." At the same time he 'knew' he had a good risk.[25]

These were the years of the making of what became the Moulton Ranch and holdings, coming to 22,000 acres. Aside from being the

---

25. Kaspare Cohn got his start by allowing shepherds to store their money in his personal safe while they traveled with their flocks, there being no banks in Los Angeles at the time. (See endnote 15: Kaspare Cohn.)

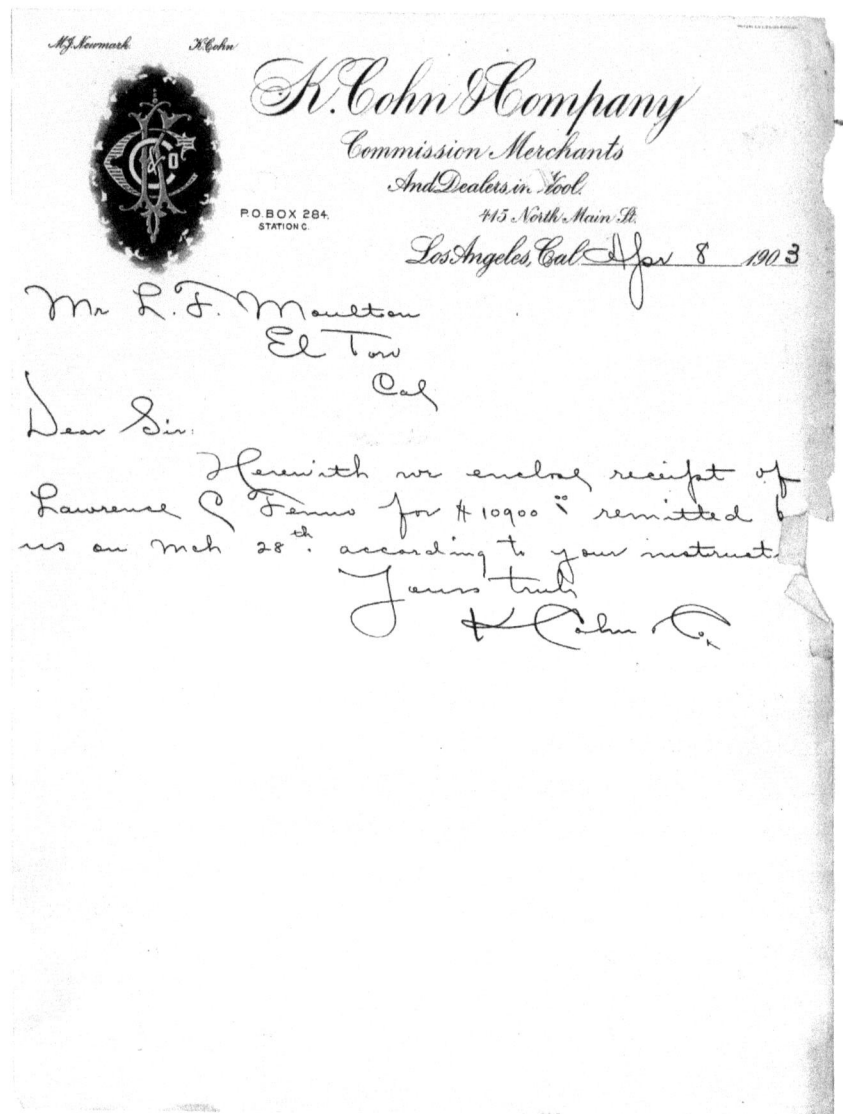

Moulton Museum's holdings include extensive correspondence between Lewis, Lawrence, and Kaspare Cohn. Text reads: Mr L. F. Moulton, El Toro, Cal, Dear Sir, Herewith our envelope receipt of Laurence C. Fenno for $10,900.00 remmitted to us on March 28th according to your interest. Yours truly, K Cohn & Co.

business head, Lewis did not hesitate, in emergency or when absolutely necessary, to take part, as he had done in its beginnings, in the physical activity end of it. It meant running sheep to the best grazing grounds,

Shearing sheep on the Moulton Ranch. Navajos traveled from ranch to ranch shearing sheep. Basques and Mexicans often completed the crew.

often long distances, to Big Bear, south to Oceanside, north to Bakersfield. It meant hiring responsible herders, these for the most part, Basques, the chuck-wagon treks to the herders' posts to bring food and supplies to both men and animals supervised. Sheep dogs had to be trained, horses broken. Obtaining the pitch for treating the sheep for ticks was an ordeal in itself, as it had to be dredged up and hauled from the La Brea tar pits, this in the environs of Los Angeles, quite a distance from the ranch. And then shearing time when the Indians, mostly

Portrait of Lewis Moulton in his early 30s, taken in Los Angeles, Calif.

Navajos, I think, would stream in, complete with squaw and papoose, to set up their tents, home base for the duration.

Together with the necessity to direct the work for the Indians, with so many grouped and thrown together, there would be some family disturbance to be appeased or clash of personalities. But the most annoying might happen on weekends. By some manner, hard to pinpoint, determine where it was obtained, demon liquor worked its havoc. Happily, not too often. However, the occasion might arise when one of them, crazed or stupefied with the stuff, would get out of control. There was one workable way to silence and sober the troublesome one—dump him in the water trough.

Lewis had many valued friendships. It was inevitable, for 'he made a good friend,' never hesitated to help where he could, quietly and without fanfare, or share. He respected the dignity of the individual. Mr. Thurston, an old-time Californian, too, once said of him, "He was a gentleman in every sense of the word."

Some of the famous were known to Lewis. Marah Ellis Ryan, poetess and author of twenty-two books was one. For both health reasons and all the better to meditate and write, Marah had ensconced herself at the Mission at Capistrano. Surrounded on all sides by sheep ranches, Indians constantly in sight, it seemed to fall into place that she become imbued with the drama of her surroundings, her book, 'Indian Love Letters' evolving as a masterpiece of sensitive portrayal in words.

Madame Helena Modjeska, the Polish actress, held almost in the same category and esteem as Bernhardt and

Lewis Moulton considered courting author Marah Ellis Ryan and asked his cousin Lawrence to look into her background. Lawrence replied, 'I find that she who writes under the name of Marah Ellis Ryan is a Mrs. S.E. Martin, who was born in 1860. I have as yet not been able to get the details of her antecedents... I do not want to discourage you from a pleasant friendship, but [] to use your own words, be wary until I can get you more complete information."

Duse, was another. She had trod the boards in many countries, giving of her 'soul and refinement'—this at a time when the profession as a whole was eyed askance. Upon retirement, her lovely home was always open to friends. She enjoyed people. She and her husband, Count Bizenta, gave many wonderful parties.[26] Still another good friend of Lewis' was Judge Egan of Capistrano.[27] I could go on.

Lewis told me of an amusing incident. This happened before I knew him. He'd received a note from the

Lewis Moulton (left)
with Judge Richard Egan.

popular novelist, Helen Hunt Jackson, asking his indulgence in the matter of her coming out to the ranch that she might do some on-the-spot researching for the book she was presently writing. The title of the book, *Ramona*. Mr. Moulton, of course, granted the courtesy, assuring her he would be pleased to have her. She arrived with entourage, complete with aides and photographer. All that day, Lewis kept from his work, taking time to make the rounds with her, often stopping the labor of the Indians so that she might arrange and take all the pictures she desired. Miss Jackson left thanking Lewis profusely for his kindness. A few weeks later, an envelope arrived in the mail with a photo enclosed, showing a shearing scene taken at his very own ranch. A bill was also rendered—one dollar due. But this probably may have been sent by the photographic service and Miss Jackson thoroughly unaware of this 'grave social error.'[28]

---

26. Helena Modjeska was the most famous person in Orange County at the time. (See endnote 16: Madame Helena Modjeska.)
27. Richard Egan was the *alcalde* of San Juan Capistrano, a term meaning "mayor, judge, and chief dignitary." (See endnote 17: Judge Egan of Capistrano.)
28. Famous today for the novel *Ramona*, Helen Hunt Jackson spent most of her years campaigning for Native American rights. (See endnote 18: Helen Hunt Jackson.)

Lewis found a wonderful sheep man and manager, a Mr. Daguerre.[29] Mr. Daguerre had been with the old Forster family, owners of large ranch holdings in Capistrano. As time went on, Lewis knew he had found a gem of a man. In spite of this, there were setbacks. With the droughts came losses, dwindling of flock, the seeping in of cattle herd trails made the need for changes almost imperative for survival. During a tough year, the two men got together in a business arrangement. They came to the conclusion it was best to go along with the new. They pooled funds. Mr. Daguerre brought in $37,000, for which amount Lewis generously granted him a third interest. His Uncle Fenno, too, did not hesitate to send him $75,000 as a loan, this debt cleared and paid for in time as set forth in the promissory note. The men proceeded to put into practice the changes they deemed necessary.

Jean Pierre Daguerre, his wife Maria Eugenia, and their children (L to R) Josephine, Domingo, Juana and Grace.

Mr. Daguerre died tragically in a ranch accident. Charlotte, our first born, was almost two years old when this happened. How he adored our little girl! He was on a wagon close to an area where an oil-drilling operation was going on. Mr. Moulton had permitted the drilling on leased land. As Mr. Daguerre neared the spot, the horses, perhaps excited

---

29. Jean Pierre Daguerre, who immigrated to the US from France, 1857–1911. (See endnote 19: Jean Pierre Daguerre & family.)

by the unfamiliar noises and commotion and people, shied and strained to such a degree that the singleton gave way and dropped, the man, reins in hand, lifted bodily and face down to fall into the groove in front of him, the wagon turning at the same time. The horses, now thoroughly frantic, one kicked up his heels to plant a blow on the helpless man's chest. Rushed to the hospital, he passed away twelve days later. A great loss. We all felt it deeply.[30]

In relating the above sad event I've gone ahead of things—now back to Mr. Moulton and myself. Though the working of the ranch was quite demanding, he found time to keep me constantly aware of his feelings and intentions toward me. I was still busy at my job, but to avoid the dreary daily long rides to work from home and then return, I had decided to move in with friends in the city. Inevitably this increased my social activity. I remember with extreme pleasure the friendship that developed between the effervescent Ozzie Ogen and me. Her enthusiasm, her zest for life were thoroughly contagious. Ozzie taught dramatics at U.C.L.A. She helped arrange and direct great entertainment programs for the Ebell Club of which we were both members. Her touch was magic. In plays, she was capable of inspiring adequate performances from the most inept or rank amateur. I think she was a genius at this sort of thing. Later she became Mrs. Hunnewell, her husband a broker dealing in stocks and bonds.

Ozzie functioned as chaperone for me when Lewis invited us out to the ranch, not only to enjoy the outing but to see how a ranch is run—the roundups—how the Indians lived. There was a guessing game they would play at sundown, something like 'button, button, who has the button?' With an older man sitting apart to make certain there would be no cheating, the men would squat

---

30. Barbara Letter, a Laguna Woods History Center volunteer, wrote that Daguerre's horses were spooked by an automobile rather than oil drilling equipment. See endnote 19: Jean Pierre Daguerre & Family.

in a circle, hands hidden under a blanket over their knees, then pass something one to the other, usually two sticks or bones, small enough to be held in a man's hand. The side that was guessing pointed quickly to the hand it thought had the marked stick or bone. If right, it was the other side's turn to do the hiding. If not, the first side had the piece again. The children's games were similar to hopscotch and hide-and-go-seek. They tried to see how far they could hop on one leg or play tag.

Lewis wasn't waiting any longer. He was now pressing his suit in earnest. With father's whole-hearted blessing and 'my permission' (as courtships go these days, I certainly took a long time), we were married at Dad's home in Oxnard, November 29th, 1908, our honeymoon destination, Hawaii.

Ozzie Ogen (left) and Nellie Gail (right) volunteering at the Laguna Beach Art Association. Nellie took en plein air classes from Association founders Anna Hills and Edgar Payne. The Association later became the Laguna Art Museum.

Lewis and Nellie Gail Moulton on their honeymoon voyage to Hawaii in 1908.

Before boarding our steamer which was docked at the San Francisco Harbor, arriving by train in that city, we paused to visit with Lewis' brother, Irving, a banker, now making his home there.[31]

The first three days at sea I was feeling like anything but a bride, but after that I was fine, fully enjoying the fun on board, the deck lounging and, coming back a seasoned sailor.

Lewis made the Hawaiian stay memorable in many ways. He was not unknown—he'd been a visitor there before and so made a good guide. I remember the surprise and warm pleasure we felt at finding the many invitations from friends and business associates of Lewis' (and Irving's) at our hotel after returning from a short sight-seeing walk in Honolulu.

---

31. Irvine Farrar Moulton, Lewis' younger brother, was born in Boston, Massachusetts on February 12, 1867. He married Anne Scholfiend and the couple had two children, Harriet and Brooks (Ancestry.com). Irving served as Vice President and Cashier for the Bank of California in San Francisco, one of the most prominent banks in the West in the late 19th and early 20th centuries ("Growth Told by Statement," San Francisco Call, Dec 20, 1903).

In the year of our marriage, Hawaii was not yet considered such a tourist's haven as it is today and many of the non-native inhabitants were of the second or third generation of the first missionaries. I would think the names Captain Cook, the explorer and navigator who first came upon the Hawaiian Islands, and Princess Kaiulani will never die, and then they were even more alive than today. Since that first sight of the Islands, I've taken at least four more trips. The natives are somehow not so native now, but this is not true of some of the other islands.

The horseback climb across old lava to view the volcano (I believe it was Mauna Loa) at as close range as possible is something I remember vividly. My new husband was taken from me! Let me explain. We had reached a four-mile point, lanterns ablaze lighting our way, the mist, the vapor with its pungent odor all around us, the horses beginning to move slowly, some of the riders dismounting to relieve and soothe the animals, when suddenly there was a little commotion. One of the women had had an accident. I cannot recall the exact details; it may have been that in getting off her horse she sprained her ankle. But whatever, the men were called upon to aid her husband, a professor at Stanford, in lifting and carrying the rather rotund lady down the return path by foot. Lewis was one. And so I had to travel the entire comeback trail of four miles solo.

A month later, on New Year's Day of 1909, the newlyweds walked down the gangplank at San Francisco. Visiting once more, briefly, with Irving, we went on to arrive at El Toro and our new home. To make a rhyme—'I began life as the rancher's wife.'

Our house, still standing at El Toro and now the home of daughter Charlotte, was being built while we were away. I had conferred with the contractor and the carpenters (architects were hard to find then) and had worked out the building plans, landscape and color scheme. Rugs were being made in Germany, furniture being put together slowly and with care, foreign purchases added.

Three mule teams pulling plows on the Moulton Ranch in 1913,
reprinted, with permission, from the historical collection of First American
Financial Corporation. All rights reserved.

Lewis wanted it to be a home to be proud of, be happy in. I made a facetious remark to him at first sight of the kitchen, something about 'it being necessary for the maid to skate from kitchen to the dining area.' Lewis took it seriously, though, and changes were made.

As I've stated, even before we were married, ranch ways were changing drastically. Grazing areas were harder and harder to find. The building boom of Southern California was creeping in. The 28,000 head of sheep were sold off gradually and more cattle brought in. There was planting of barley, beans, mostly the black-eyed variety, some wheat, although here there was the problem of cutting before mildew, more grain, alfalfa to feed the horses. The building of the Santa Fe coming through from Los Angeles to San Diego had opened up communities. Mexicans now flowed in to do the harvesting, as well as Indians. Men were needed for the threshing machines, which were still pulled by mule teams or horses.

L. F. Moulton & Company packing house with barley ready for shipping located near present-day Sand Canyon Ave. and Freeway 5.

Two cookhouses were installed on the ranch, these in constant activity, for large quantities of food had to be prepared, the great caldrons simmering away, the ovens, at all times, wafting their delicious aroma of freshly baked bread. Another building held bunks for the men.

Mr. Moulton now simply occupied himself with the directing of operations. An office was established, daily records carefully kept. It was 'L. F. Moulton & Company.' A CPA from the city came regularly once a month. A daughter of Mr. Daguerre helped in the office.[32]

At home we had new members in the family. Charlotte came along in 1910. How pleased and happy Lewis was at the advent of the birth. Then Louise, our tomboy. Daddy was the indulgent one— mother inherited the role of disciplinarian.

Lewis was a man of order and habit, and also sensitive to the feelings of those around him. He would rise very early in the morning, pause to read a few passages of the Bible, then set out to the cookhouse to have breakfast with the men and to lay out the work program. In being with the ranch help in the beginning of the day, he regarded the ritual as an inspirational procedure reaching out not only to the men but himself as well. He was

---

32. The children of Jean Pierre Daguerre and Marie E. Duguet were Domingo, Juanita, Grace, and Josephine. Likely Nellie is referring to Juanita here, because she refers to Josephine as "another of Daguerre's daughters" later in the text. However, this might refer to Josephine, who worked as the company secretary and manager for many years.

much admired, a compassionate employer, available and on hand to be helpful in any emergency.

As much as Lewis never talked about his problems outside the home, there was one time when he could not hide his worry—something vastly important was disturbing him. He discussed it with me, but I knew it was a situation he had to decide for himself. The board of the Union Bank had put out a tempting proposition. It was that he sell out entirely to the corporation for a certain sum. They had approached him with the deal and presented it to Lewis in terms of 'You've worked hard—why not give it up—we will give you all this money—go abroad—travel with the family—have a good time—no further responsibilities!' Lewis came back from the conference in Los Angeles looking thoughtful, silent, debating it all in his mind. I waited, feeling for him and with him. He was restless, sleepless all night. The next morning all disquietude was gone—he had made an unalterable decision—not to sell!

Nellie with her firstborn, Charlotte, in 1910.

Nellie with Charlotte (bow in hair) and Louise, the tomboy, circa 1915.

Portrait with Louise, Nellie Gail, Charlotte and Lewis around 1920.

The ranch kept growing, more productive every day. It also needed every attention. This did not phase Lewis; after all, he'd practically grown up in these surroundings. He liked to see progress but never beyond the point of conscience. I don't remember his having any lawsuits, or enemies. He enjoyed the theatre. We traveled together on a

Lewis in a carriage in front of the main ranch house, circa 1915.

Louise Moulton Hanson started riding horses at a young age, taught by her father.

few trips with the children, but later he rather encouraged and allowed me to do some journeying on my own, in fact, traveling the world over. Truly, his work was his hobby, his hobby his work.

Lewis was not a joiner. He became a member of the Jonathon Club but hardly attended. It took him twenty-five years to finally be persuaded to become an Elk. He loved Charlotte and Louise dearly, took pleasure in them, constantly bought them gifts. Christmas was always a big and happy occasion, all of us going to church together, merrily driving down the Santa Ana Canyon. This was around 1915, the road not yet paved.

The years passed quickly. The ranch was now almost all cattle. The girls were now young women. Both received their degrees from Pomona College—Charlotte in 1930, Louise in 1936. Charlotte became a bride two years after graduation. Louise made it four years later.

Louise was married in a very formal, large wedding and reception. It was a lovely affair, held at the gardens of our ranch home. There was one sad note—Lewis was ailing and not able to see his own daughter wed.

Lewis passed away in December, 1938. He left his heart and the labor of his work with us. In his will, he deeded one-third each to his girls, Charlotte, Louise and myself.

Time dulls the pain of grief, suspends it as it were, for the daily exigencies of life demand attention. Once more I found myself working in an office. With the help of Josephine, another of Mr. Daguerre's daughters, I took on the management of the ranch. I did this for twelve years. The one taking the reins and following in her father's footsteps was Louise. She was a child of the outdoors, loved all animals, rode a horse like a champion horsewoman (a bona fide one today) and, after taking a course in husbandry, an efficient ranchwoman in her own right.

Eventually there were the land sales, the housing developments, and so the creation of Laguna Niguel and Leisure World.[33]

---

33. The Rancho which Lewis Moulton purchased from Cyrus Rawson and made the foundation of Moulton Ranch was earlier named Rancho Niguel. (See endnote 20: Laguna Niguel.)

CHRISTMAS GREETING.
TO OUR WORTHY NEIGHBOR
LEWIS F. MOULTON.

If the Test of Life is nothing less
Than Actual neighborly helpfulness,
Then Neighbor Moulton hath a part
Secure within The Public's heart.
For lo! he shares with lavish hand
The largess of his leagues of land;
Content to serve The Common Good
And welfare of his neighborhood.
Till now, his name's a synonym
For all those Traits we've found in him,
Kindliness, and Brotherhood
And silent ways of doing good;
"A loaning folks a Team of mules
With seed, and feed and farming tools;
Till scores of poor discouraged men
Have Taken heart to start again,
And win, through faith, and kindliness
A goodly measure of success."
What wonder with our Christmas Cheer
We laud this well loved Pioneer
Who through his days hath always stood
For Helpfulness and Brotherhood.

Lombardy Lane 1931.   Isaac J. Frazee.

*Lewis always had a good rapport with his neighbors. Lombardy Lane
and Isaac J. Frazee penned this in his honor in 1931.*

All of Me

PART III

MY TRAVELS
AROUND THE WORLD

I would say it might be best to start this short and quick account of my travels by mentioning my 'first flying trip.' That was when I was literally thrown out of mother's arms in the terrible cyclone in Irving, Kansas.

My next trip—by train—the time father took up government land in western Kansas. Then Horace, the building of the frame structure, father hopefully intending to establish himself, all soon turning to ashes with the advent of the stolen votes in favor of Tribune. Following that, the trek across Kansas in the covered wagon with father and Alta—and back to Hebron.

I was only ten when mother put me on the train to travel alone to visit grandfather.

The happiest sojourn—with father and mother and Carrie to the World's Fair in Chicago. The saddest, Carrie and I on our way to Covina, California, to stay with Alta after mother's passing—this just a year later, in 1894. Back to Hebron on the Santa Fe with father at Thanksgiving time, the year 1895. To Business College in Omaha and subsequent return to Hebron to teach at the rural school in Thayer County.

As an independent young woman; that interesting trip to Gallup, New Mexico and on to Los Angeles, California to visit members of the family—1902. To Wenatchee, Washington after the visit for the

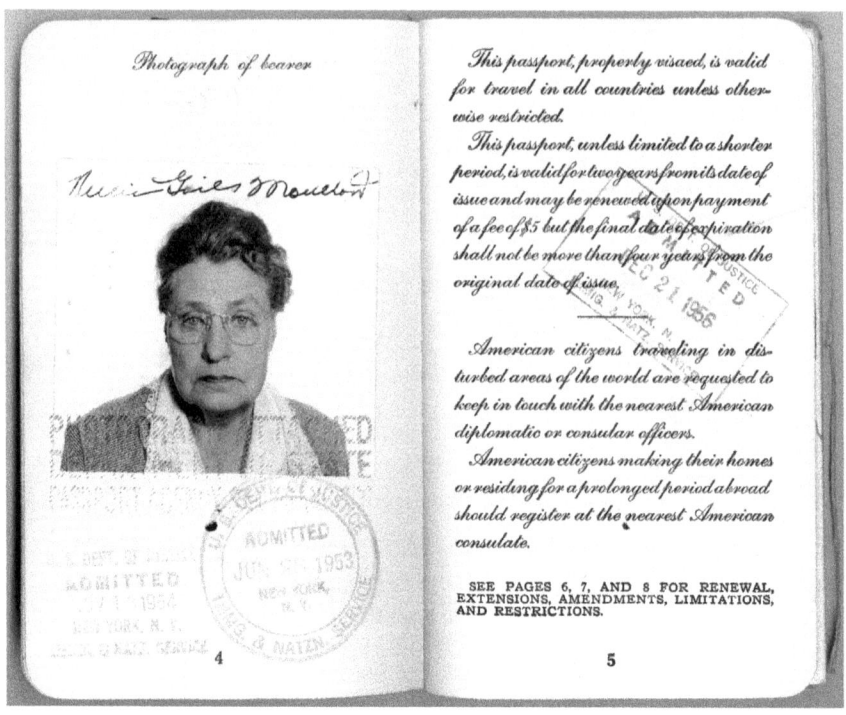

Washington State Examinations and to take up my new teaching assignment at Lake Chelan.

And then—1903—traveling to El Toro, California, to see father and there to meet Mr. Moulton.

To Port Orchard, Washington, my next teaching post—from there, Seattle, as principal at the Dunlap School. Vacation time—training south to father, now living in Monita, California. With the beginning of the school term at hand—the big decision—to resign and remain in California—this the fall of 1905.

November 29th, 1908, I married Lewis Fenno Moulton and set off to Hawaii for our wedding trip, the first for me away from these shores.

* * *

It was in 1913 that Lewis and I, with three-year-old baby daughter, Charlotte, ventured a trip East, primarily to meet Lewis' relatives in Boston but making many stops in between. Nurse-assistant Nellie Blivin traveled with us. Members of the family I remember particularly were Bradley and Ed Fenno; also the branch of the family owning the firm Fenno & Shaw, holding heavy interests in copper mines.

We had started out by way of New Orleans and New York, to return via Hebron and Chicago, but not immediately, for little Charlotte fell ill and had to be hospitalized. Daddy had to leave us for business reasons, Annette Goheen, my best friend, coming down from Evanston to see Lewis off with me at the depot.

Louise was about a year old when I attended the Fair in San Francisco, at the same time visiting with Mr. Moulton's brother and his wife, Annie and Irving Moulton. This was 1915. World War I now on in Europe.

*Nellie with her girls on their way to the Ebell Club in Santa Ana
in the family's 1922 Cadillac Suburban Touring Sedan.*

Verso in Nellie's handwriting reads: Calif. Federated Clubs 1920 Convention held in Yosemite Valley. This group picture represents the Santa Ana Calif. Ebell Club in the pageant at Yosemite where 1500 club women attended. This note added on 1967 in my old home at 22762 Vista de Sol Laguna Beach, 40 years later.

In 1921, as a member of the Ebell Club, I attended the State Federation of Clubs Conference at Yosemite National Park.[34]

In 1923, when Charlotte was thirteen, there was a trip to Alaska.

And then, 1928, the three-month tour of Europe with Annette (the idea for the trip having germinated long before, in 1913, during our get-together in Chicago).[35] We started by train, going north to Montreal, Canada, then boarding an English boat to travel 1,000

---

34. The "International Academy for the Advancement of Women," later renamed "Ebell Society" after its founder, Dr. Adrian John Ebell, offered cultural, intellectual, and industrial opportunities for women. Its first site opened in Oakland, California. (See endnote 21: Ebell Club in Los Angeles.)

35. See endnote 22: Annette Galbraith Goheen.

miles out to sea on the St. Lawrence River, meeting icebergs along the way. Then the second boat. France was our first country halt—Paris, of course. Then Switzerland, Germany, England. In Italy we viewed the galleries in Florence, saw Genoa, the birthplace of Columbus, Florence to Pisa, Naples and Venice, not forgetting the gondola ride with serenading gondolier. Rome—verily the Eternal City—St. Peter's, the Vatican Museum, Trevi Fountain, stopping at one of those Via Veneto sidewalk cafes.

In 1936, Louise and I took an Orient tour. This was her college graduation gift. Boarding the Japanese boat, Hiye Maru, in Seattle, we sailed to arrive at the first port of call, Yokohama. Then by ship, rail and motor, we touched many places to visit and enjoy. Naming a few—Kamakura, Tokyo and the Imperial Palace. From Tokyo, a two-hour train ride to arrive at Nikko, alpine splendor of the Orient, to visit the Toshogu Shrines, architectural wonders. A flight by night over Formosa and Okinawa to Hong

One of Nellie's letters to Lewis when she was traveling. Letter reads:
Hello "Daddy"! - A very pleasant Sunday morning. All having a delightful outing. Wish
you were here too. Will soon be home now. Much love from your own family. Nellie

Kong, its amazing, beautiful and busy harbor, the walks through its teeming streets, the shops with irresistible wares, and prices. Canton, the home of the great University, the Thieves Market, the sampans filling the river and canals, these the very living quarters of most of the populace there. An authentic native dinner at the home of a person of prominence. And Kyoto, still with the look of something out of the past century, visiting the Heian Shrine, its pond and garden, this built in 1895, a breathtakingly beautiful and colorful sight. The Nijo Castle, representing the fine art of these people, and everywhere school children, all in orderly procession, taking in and absorbing the beauty and history of their land, just as we were.

In 1939 Louise and I took another trip together. This time East to Boston, then Chicago to view the World's Fair going on that year.[36]

The year 1947—going South American Way. Our itinerary included Caracas, capital city of Venezuela. It lies between inland and coastal mountain ranges; on the coast side, its vistas and shores so similar to our southern California, as is its climate. It sprawls for miles, has many high-rise office and apartment buildings, shopping centers and districts. Lima, capital of Peru, land of the ancient Incas, its Archeological Museum vividly retelling in displays this fascinating period of history. The spectacular flight over the snow-capped Andes cannot be forgotten. Rio de Janeiro, once the capital of Brazil, a beautiful, busy and modern city, the coastline view uncluttered, the sands of its Copacabana Beach truly golden, and, most awe-inspiring, the statue of the Christ at the peak of Hunchback Mountain. On the boat to Rio there was an interesting gentleman who had been President of Brazil, exiled first to Europe, then Portugal. He was returning to his homeland after seven years.

---

36. Probably Nellie means the World's Fair in New York City. (See endnote 23: World's Fair NYC.)

An avid photographer who preferred 35mm slides,
Nellie took this photo of a Peruvian native in 1947.

As the boat docked crowds of excited citizens, as well as dignitaries, were on hand to give him a rousing welcome.[37]

Buenos Aires, capital of Argentina, built to a chessboard pattern on an expanse of flatland, to countryside and pampas. The city, a lively metropolis, one of the largest in Argentina, with wide streets, elegant shops and busy waterfront, has a greater mark of the cultural in aspect rather than the commercial. There are many libraries, the great Colon Opera House, filled to capacity at every performance; and its immense Palermo Park has a setting of myriads of statues and monuments, tribute to their historical background.

---

37. In 1930, Getúlio Vargas, a Brazilian revolutionary leader defeated in Brazil's election that year, led an armed coup and deposed the sitting president Washington Luis Pereira de Sousa. President Sousa was exiled for 17 rather than 7 years.

1953—the first trip around the world with the Clarks.[38] First port of call, Honolulu once again, the Wake Island, Tokyo, Kyoto, Bangkok, Singapore, and Manila, center of the young republic of the Philippines. We'd been told beforehand of the wonderful bargains we would find in this city but, arriving on a Sunday, we were all disappointed to find all shops closed. The people are deeply religious—it is their day of rest and prayer. However, there were enough interesting sights—the Malacanang Palace, Intramuros, the Spanish walled city, Fort Santiago and the University district.

India—a land where you really see something 'that's different.' Stretching over two-thousand miles, the country offers a rich variety of soil, scenery and sights, faces and places. Of more than ordinary interest are her ancient and modern cities, lakes and gardens, temples and mosques, monuments and memorials, centers of industry and seats of education. We here in the United States have been given such a wrong overall concept of the country. It is not all camels and cows straying across the roads. Of the places we touched: Jaipur, Old Delhi, seat of seven successive empires, the burial place of Ghandi—adjoining and part of it, New Delhi, superbly laid out capital of India, built by Sir Edwin Lutyens, the famous British architect, and inaugurated in 1931. The flight to Kashmir reached by plane from Delhi, bringing you almost to the foot of the Himalaya range. Ceylon, jutting out into the Indian Ocean, with its miles of beautiful coastline, a paradise for native and tourist. All of the land houses temples, mosques and tombs conveying the magnificence of Muslim architecture and sculpture. Christians are mostly found in the coastal areas and in the south, Goa, a place of pilgrimage. The Church of Bom Jesus in Goa contains the embalmed remains of St. Francis Xavier. The 16th-century Roman Catholic cathedral of St. Thome in Madras

---

38. We don't know whom she is referring to, but in the Flight Journal she mentions the trip is "conducted by Dr Clarke tours." "Clark" or "Clarke" might refer to a tour company rather than family name.

is likewise an object of veneration. Calcutta, another teaming city, a visit to its Jain Temple and the Victoria Museum. Bombay, capital of Maharashtra, a metropolitan city that immediately makes you feel at home. Here you see something of the Hindu upper classes, highly civilized, the women in dazzling costumes, their beauty set off by a red spot on the forehead and sometimes by a precious stone in the left nostril. The first point of interest is the Gateway of India, a kind of triumphal arch. There's the beauty of the Hanging Gardens at Malabar Hill, the Flora Fountain in the middle of town, and also its famous zoo where children can have camel and elephant rides.

To Athens, Greece, to visit the Plaka district, the port of Piraeus, the houses of Parliament, the Tomb of the Unknown Soldier, the Parthenon, the Royal Palace.

To Istanbul, Turkey, where our group of three ladies, including myself, visited four nightclubs one evening, the pièce de rèsistance in entertainment at each, a bevy of scantily clad belly dancers. After being mesmerized with such antics, going out into the streets made one sharply aware of the contrast in adornment of the average woman, for a great many still kept the custom of veiled faces. Our guide for this 'evening of dissipation' had been a most knowledgeable and charming gentleman. Later, we learned that this ingratiating fellow had been a former spy, a member of the underground, feeding information to the Germans in World War II, against the British. Apparently he was clever enough to get out in time. From the looks of him, average height, average in features, one would never suspect him of such intrigue.

Cairo, Egypt. The Egyptian coastline seems at first regular and tubular and then flashes into view all sorts of extraordinary peaks, all equally sharp and bare. At sunset, the western coast draws to itself all the beauty of the evening; as the sun disappears, the mountains, until then covered in mist, begin to pass through every possible shade of violet from the very deepest to the most transparent mauve.

Nellie painting Niagra Falls on one of her many trips.

In 1954—the African sojourn. Places we visited—Mombasa, Zanzibar, Capetown, Johannesburg, Nairobi, the capital of Kenya. Addis Ababa, Ethiopia, and invited to a tea reception at the palace of Emperor Haile Selassie. We'd been coached as to protocol, to approach His Majesty in groups of four, bow in greeting, then withdraw, never turning. Some, in their excitement, completely forgot their instructions—a few backs were quite in evidence to His Majesty.[39]

To touch Algiers, Casablanca, Marakesch, the capital of Morocco.

To Israel: Tel Aviv and Jaffa, a crowded city—here much excavation goes on. To Massada, towering above the Dead Sea, to Bethlehem, visiting the Church of the Nativity, then to arrive at the ancient city of Jerusalem. By motorcoach, to ascend the Mount of Olives, later to tour the city along the path of Via Dolorosa to the Church of the Holy Sepulchre, via Jezreel Valley to Nazareth to visit the Christian shrines.

Brother Cyrus came with me on my second trip around the world. This included flying to the Fiji Islands, to Australia, New Zealand. We were gone fourteen weeks.

---

39. Ethiopia's Emperor Haile Selassie is closely associated with Rastafarianism. (See endnote 24: Emperor Haile Selassie/Rastafarianism)

I took my old friend Anette to Hawaii in 1960. It had changed considerably. The modern elements had wrought their influence.

I have touched just briefly on the history of my travels, leaving out a great deal—what I have forgotten is all to be seen in vivid and minute portrayal in my extensive file of slide films.

My next trip is yet to be.

FINALE

*A*s the last word is written here, I am no longer at the Leisure World apartment. For more than a year now I've been at my Three Arch Bay Home in South Laguna, this at the top of the hill, tranquil and cheerful with the wonderful view of the ocean. It was something I needed in this sundown of my life. Four months ago I celebrated, with a party, my 90th birthday. I had many of my family attending, the very young, the older and the much older. When they left and the house was still, the laughter, the words spoken, the outpouring of sentiment still hummed in my brain. And again it was time to float down the shadowy wings of thought.

In the gamut of my years, I've traversed with Father Time all the incredible advances the new to the world take so casually. As a little girl, I crossed the midwestern plains in a covered wagon. Last year, watching a thing called television, I witnessed man's first step on the surface of the moon.

I have seen so many 'firsts.' The first telephone, the first gaslight, the first use of electricity, the first typewriter, the first bicycle, the first car, the first plane, one of the first women to work in an office. Skirts were still in fashion—men were permitted the enjoyment of using a little imagination. The preservation of the family was a tradition to honor and revere. The Gay Nineties were gay only because the promise of freedoms of the sexes was simply an affectation and not a reality. I wish we had stayed that way. Attending the opera, the theatre, a late supper was the 'fun thing to do.' I was there and aware of the first rumblings of the suffrage movement. When women were finally given their right to vote, I was one of the first to cast my vote—for Woodrow Wilson—not knowing that war would soon be our lot.

I recall those war songs:
"Over There, Over There"
"Ka-Ka-Ka-Katie"
"Pack Up Your Troubles in Your Old Kit Bag"
"Keep Home Fires Burning While Hearts are Yearning"
"How Can You Keep Them Down on the Farm After
      They've Seen Paree"

The Happy songs:
"Only a Bird in a Gilded Cage"
"After the Ball"
"A Hot Time in the Old Town Tonight"
"When You Were Sweet Sixteen"
"Champagne Garden"[40]

These remembrances I have told, gathered to put in words, are not all my tender memories—some are too sacred and private and I wish

---

40. These are the titles of songs composed between 1891–1918. (See endnote 25: Song Titles)

to keep them within my own heart. I have only desired to touch on the human elements, bits and pieces, presenting a scene or two that, though seeming trivial, catapulted me to meet my destiny—and also that you may know the real Lewis Fenno Moulton, a man of faith and sense of decency, who bore through life the white flower of a Christian gentleman.

In the legacy left to me, in the name of my husband, in memory of his humanitarianism, I have endeavored, in my donations to community projects, to help, to (hopefully) encourage the spirit of creativeness and enjoyment of the arts, for there is one thing I believe will never fade into oblivion—beauty in literature, painting, music, the drama—no matter how some, for whatever motive, will agitate to bring true talent to ridicule—those who appreciate and know its worth will never let it die.

—Nellie Gail Moulton
March, 1970

BONUS MATERIAL

"FLIGHT JOURNAL"
by Nellie Gail Moulton

Editor's Note

*N*ellie Gail loved traveling and considered her trips to be an important part of her story, not only the voluntary touristy voyages, but also those "flights" imposed on her by circumstances.

This brief journal summarizes Nellie's most impactful trips. The original, handwritten document (preserved at the Moulton Museum) contains numerous misspellings and grammatical errors. For example, most instances of "flight" were spelled "flyte," and Charlotte, Nellie's oldest daughter, was often spelled "Charlott." This inconsistency is very different from the punctilious manuscript of *Living Memories*.

Nellie with daughter Charlotte (Mathis) and granddaughter Jane (Barnes).

A penciled note at the bottom from daughter Charlotte (Moulton) Mathis reads, "This is not in Mother's handwriting—and she did not check the spelling!" ~ CMM 6/13/83

Most likely Nellie Gail dictated the journal to one of her caregivers. Despite the issues with form, in substance the journal appears accurate. I have corrected only enough errors to aid understanding.

Scott T. Barnes

Damage in Irving, Kansas after the tornado of 1880.
Courtesy Kansas University Archives.

My first flight

I was born in Irving Kansas in a two-story house. At the age of seven months we had a terrible cyclone. Mother was holding me in front of our living room window, watching the cyclone approach, then it hit the house and broke the large window we were standing in front of. The force picked up mother and I and carried us through the room into the bedroom and set us on the bed unharmed. This was my first flight. This was only a stopover. Father was trying to get us out of the house, but all the doors were jammed, but he finally managed to break through one of the doors and got us out. We no more got outside when the cyclone picked me out of mother's arms, throwing me quite a number of feet into a rock pile. Father and mother rushed over to rescue me. They thought I was dead; I was white and full of blood, which proved to be mother's blood, as she was badly cut from the broken window. As in all things, the cyclone passed on, leaving desolation in its path. Eighty-one people were killed from this cyclone, so we were very fortunate.

Photo of Greeley Train Station, reproduced with permission from Anderson County Historical Society, Garnett, Kansas

My 2nd flight

Father and mother moved to West Kansas near the Colorado border line near the small town of Greeley. Father invested in a quarter section of land on which he built a sod house, plastering the inside and outside, which made the house cool in the summer and warm in the winter.

He purchased a pair of beautiful black horses. When everything was completed he sent for us and we took the train to Greeley, which was my second flight.

Here father farmed for one year, planting fruit trees, raising vegetables and large watermelons, some weighing as much as 50 lbs.

This was not a profitable operation and he left the farm and we moved to Horace Kansas, which was my third flight.[41]

3rd flight

We had hardly settled in our new environment than mother contracted Typhoid fever and was at the verge of death, but eventually recovered.

---

41. Actually, Horace borders Colorado, while Greeley lies close to Kansas City.

There were rumors that Horace was to become the county seat but [it was] in competition with another town called Tribune. But father was certain Horace would be picked, because the railroad was supposed to go through it, so he started a mercantile store.

To father's dismay, the railroad picked Tribune, and of course this town was picked for the county seat.

This finished father's business and [he] was forced to decide on another move to a more favorable location.

He purchased a covered wagon and loaded all our belongings in it and started east.

4th flight

Father put mother and my baby sister on the train, and he and I started on the trip in the covered wagon to Irving Kansas.

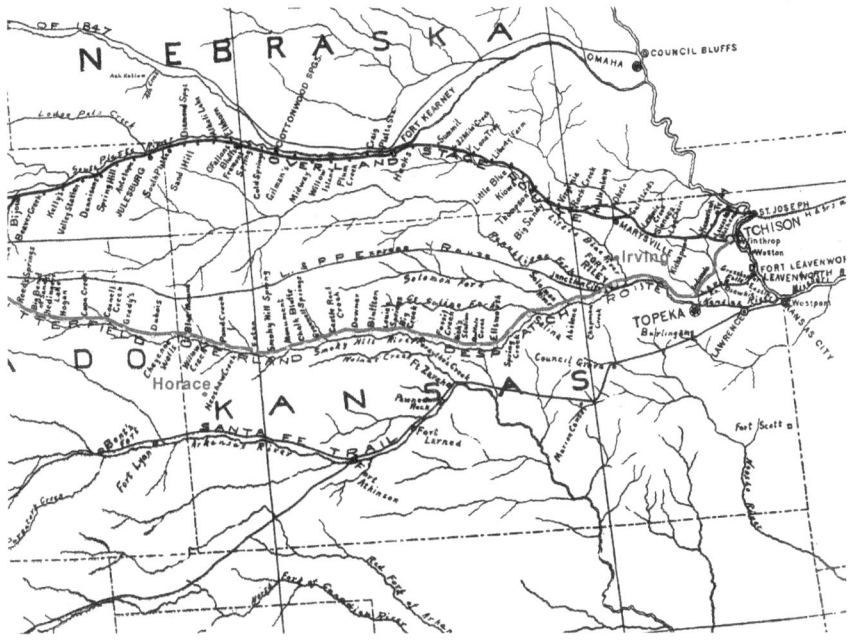

Map of Kansas with established wagon trails marked. Nellie and her father traveled much of the 450 miles from Horace to Irving off trail.

This was an experience for me, a rugged trip to say the least. One incident I recall when we were out several days, two suspicious characters followed us, and father was getting worried about them, fearing they were horse thieves or just plain robbers. When we encamped for the night, father faced the wagon west, hoping the men would think we were going in that direction.

He kept a vigil all night over the horses and our wagon. But [to] his surprise, one of the horses had been cut loose, but father called and the horse returned. We finally lost the men in question and were very much relieved.

We completed my 4th flight and arrived in Irving safely.

Nellie photographed at William Griffith photo studio in Hebron, Nebraska circa 1890.

5th flight

There was nothing of a prospect in Irving so father decided to go to his sister in Nebraska again. All of us rode the wagon for my 5th flight.

We stayed with his sister until father found something to do. His decision was to go into the contracting business with his brother, building some of the nicest homes in the city of Hebron, Thayer County. One of the nicest homes he built for us, a six-room house and a cyclone cellar for food storage and protection, so we would not [again] experience our plight of my first flight.

Here things went well for us.

6th flight

When I was at the age of 10 years, father put me on the train to visit my grandmother and grandfather all by myself for my sixth flight. This was a thrilling experience for me and instilled in me a certain amount of independence.

7th flight

In 1893, father took all of us to the World's Fair in Chicago. This was a great adventure for me and it was here that I got interested in painting; I was so enraptured with the art exhibit, I decided I wanted to learn to paint. My sister Alta was taking painting lessons at the time, so when we returned I sat at her side whenever she painted and copied her works. This was the beginning of my interest in painting which followed me through life, finally giving up when I was 80 years old.

8th flight

At the age of fifteen, I went to California, to San Gabriel, where Alta was living in hopes this climate would arrest her T.B. My little

Image of San Gabriel River at Duarte, circa 1895.
Courtesy California State Library

Postcard of Hebron Highschool circa 1900.

sister [Carrie] accompanied me on this 8th flight; she went free as the conductor never collected for her fare.

At Reno, Nevada, they removed our car from the train, and we became frantic as all our belongings were in the coach, but upon inquiring, we found out they were just rearranging the coaches and switching cars.

We stayed in California two years, and during this time mother passed away from the Grippe (flu today) and left father with us two children.

9th flight

After two years in California where I spent two terms in high school, after several visits to us by father, he decided to take us back home for my 9th flight.

I stayed at home until I graduated from high school. I was too young to teach school, so I entered a seminary and received my teaching certificate and taught in the grammar school in Hebron, teaching 51 students.

Father decided to go to Chelan, Washington.

10th flight

I decided to go to Washington with him and taught school there.

Father established a water system in Chelan and later went into the mercantile business with a partner, which was soon dissolved due to an unfaithful partner.

My school was out of the city, so I roomed and

One room school house where Nellie taught in Port Orchard, WA. Courtesy Kitsap Historical Society.

boarded with friends while teaching. When the school term was over, I was offered a teaching position in Chelan, but only taught one year as

father decided to go to Southern California to El Toro where he started the little country store there that was still in operation until 1969 when the freeway went through this property.[42]

11th flight

After leaving Chelan I took up a teaching

Dunlap School in the suburbs of Seattle where Nellie served as principal. Photo courtesy Museum of History and Industry

position in Port Orchard, Washington, rooming with other teachers. I only taught here one year and was offered a teaching job in Seattle.

42. See endnote 12, El Toro & El Toro Store, for more information.

12th flight

I moved to Seattle, in actuality a small suburb, where I was made principal of the grammar school. Later, I was appointed principal of the overall grammar schools in Seattle proper.

I held this position for one year.

13th flight

During vacations, I went to see father at El Toro, where I helped him in his bookkeeping. Here I met Mr. Moulton who was a customer of father's.

Photo of Nellie as secretary.

While in El Toro, I resigned my position from the school in Washington.

My sister Alta was going to a music conservatory, and I also was offered a scholarship by a Canadian friend, but this fell through when he failed to return from Canada.

I was offered a position in Los Angeles as a secretary, which I accepted.

Mr. Moulton kept close track of me, and I finally agreed to marry him, being married in my father's home in Moor Park[43] in 1905 with only the family and a few close friends in attendance.

---

43. Probably Moorpark, near Ventura, California.

*Photo by Nellie of Lewis Moulton during their honeymoon
in front of the Alexander Young Hotel, Honolulu.*

14th flight

After the wedding, we took a train to San Francisco where we boarded the ship for a honeymoon to Hawaii.

This was the ultimate of my flights to this period of my life. A beautiful sea voyage, wonderful weather. Upon arrival in Honolulu, we stayed at the Alexander Young Hotel which was just opened and a lovely hotel.

After touring this Paradise Island for thirty days, we returned to the mainland and to the new home Mr. Moulton had built on the ranch, and still is standing, in which my daughter Charlotte lives.[44]

15th

After my honeymoon, we settled down in our new home, so as far as traveling, there was a period of inactivity, with getting our home

---

44. Unfortunately, the Moulton ranch headquarters has since been torn down. Its current address would be near Highway 5 and 24301 Avenida de la Carlota, Laguna Hills, the avenue being named after Charlotte (Moulton) Mathis. A nearby street named for Charlotte's sister Louise is Calle de la Louisa.

Annette Goheen (Nellie's friend) on left, her son holding the ball; Nellie with Charlotte on right, likely taken in Evanston, Illinois.

furnished and all the things a new bride must do, and then in 1910 our first child Charlotte was born. When Charlotte was three years old, Mr. Moulton took us with a governess to Boston. We stopped off in New Orleans for two days, then on to Washington, D.C. for a short stay, and on to Boston where Mr. Moulton came from, visiting relatives and friends of his.

We stopped off in Chicago, where I visited Annette Goheen, my old school chum, who lived in Evanston. To this day, we still correspond frequently. Mr. Moulton left us in Chicago and went back to California.

After our visit in Evanston, we went on to Nebraska, where I came from, visiting relatives and friends. Here, Charlotte became ill, and [we] had to put her in the hospital for treatment. When she was better we went on west, but in Ogden, Utah, we had to see a doctor. We took the shortcut home through Las Vegas instead of San Francisco which our original plans called for.

After arriving home our family doctor got Charlotte well.

16th

Mr. Moulton had much business to conduct in Los Angeles so he
maintained a room permanently at
the Alexandria Hotel for nine years.

On one of his trips to Los Angeles he took Charlotte and me. This
was a thrill for Charlotte to stay in
a hotel and eat in the dining room.

Mr. Moulton was always very
proud of our children and especially
on this trip when we ate in the dining room, Charlotte gave the waiter
her order for her complete meal
which amazed Mr. Moulton—and
more so when we found she had the
menus upside down.

17th

In 1914, Louise was born, and when
she was one year old, Mr. Moulton
sent me to the San Francisco World's
Fair, leaving the two children with a
governess we had for nine years.

The Fair was a great display and I
enjoyed it immensely.

18th

On my 18th flight Mr. Moulton
and I went to Chicago, leaving the

*Postcard of Alexandria Hotel,
Los Angeles, where Lewis Moulton
kept a room.*

*Pamphlet for the San Francisco
World's Fair, courtesy California
Historical Society.*

girls with the governess. Here we visited my friend Annette. While visiting her, Mr. Moulton suggested the two of us take a European trip and he would pay both our way.

Nellie's painting of Forest Glen, Illinois.

He always wanted to keep me happy and wanted me to travel, he didn't care about traveling as he had done so much of it in his life. My friend evidently didn't think he was serious about this as she was so surprised when I sent her a night telegram telling her all arrangements had been made and the date of our departure.

19th

In 1928 I took the train to Chicago and picked my friend Annette Goheen up in Evanston. Charlotte had preceded me the year before with a group to Europe and Louise just didn't care to go, so Daddy assured me all would be well at home and for me to go.

This painting of an Italianate scene was gifted to Annette Goheen by Nellie Gail.

We left Chicago and stopped off in Detroit a day and on to Montreal, Canada, where we boarded a Canadian ship to France. We took a night train to Paris and from here started our 3-month trip of Europe conducted by Dr Clarke tours.

We visited Italy, Switzerland, Germany, Denmark, Norway, England and Scotland.

Left Liverpool by ship to New York. A wonderful trip and found all was well at home when I arrived.

20th

In 1921, the California Federation of Women's Clubs had a convention in Yosemite, so I attended this as a delegate and enjoyed beautiful Yosemite with all its grandeur and the beautiful waterfalls. A large pageant of the history of Indians was given outdoors for the 1,500 women who attended.

An avid photographer, Nellie took this photo of Yosemite Falls during her California Federation of Women's Clubs trip.

21st

In 1931, Mr. Moulton and I took a trip through the Panama Canal to New York, on to Washington, D.C. We took a train from Washington to Miami, Florida, the first and only time I was ever in Florida. From here we took a ship to Cuba and enjoyed this island very much. From Cuba we went back through the Panama Canal again and home.

This was Mr. Moulton's last trip.

An unsigned Nellie painting of Yosemite Falls.

Nellie took this photo of Atlantic City's Boardwalk
when she and Lewis traveled through there in 1931.

22nd

While on our trip through the Canal, we met some very nice friends and made out with them to take a trip to Alaska through the inland passage. So in 1932, Charlotte, who was 22 at this time, and I drove our car to Seattle and left the car there and boarded the steamer, visiting all the important little cities along the inland passages. This was an interesting trip.

23rd

A promotional image of the S.S. Siberia
from Nellie's collection of postcards.

Charlotte graduated from Pomona College in 1930 and was married in 1932. Louise graduated from the same college in 1936.

Kobe Japan

Nellie sketched Kobe, Japan during her trip.

For her graduation present I took her to the Orient.

We left from Vancouver B.C. with a large group, among whom were several professors from USC who gave very interesting lectures on board ship to the Orient. We were greeted by Japanese officials on our arrival in Tokyo.

Our tour of Japan was very extensive, covering Yokohama, Kyoto the old capital, Nara and Kobe. From Kobe we crossed the inland sea to Busan, Korea, then traveled by rail to Seoul, then into China to Mukden, to the north province of Harbin returning south to Peiching (Peking), on to Nanjing and Shanghai.

We left China by ship to Hong Kong and the Philippine Islands. From there we returned home on our ship via Honolulu.

24th

In 1938, Mr. Moulton passed away and we all missed him as he was a wonderful husband and father.

In 1939, Louise and I went east to Boston to visit Mr. Moulton's relatives and friends. After our visits were completed, we took a train to Flint, Michigan where we picked up a new Buick automobile.

My friend Annette drove back with us to California and we arrived home for Thanksgiving.

25th

In 1947, I took a South American trip conducted by Dr. and Mrs. Campbell.

Leaving on Dec 1st, we visited Panama, flying to Bogota, Colombia, Guatemala City, on to Sao Paulo, to Rio de Janeiro, Brasilia, to Ecuador. We flew over the Andes Mountains to Iquitos [Peru] then to Lima and Santiago. Most of the land tours were by bus, which took us to Buenos Aires where we spent Christmas day.

We left Buenos Aires by air to Montevideo, Uruguay. From here we flew home.

Nellie's photograph of her ship arriving at Balboa, Panama.

Diamond Head, Hawaii, photograph by Nellie Gail Moulton.

26th

In 1950, my friend Annette and I took a two-week vacation trip to Hawaii.

We enjoyed this very much. What a change since my honeymoon here, so many new hotels and new buildings, but the beautiful scenery of the islands unspoiled.

27th

In 1953, I left on the SS Wilson for an around-the-world trip.

Our first stop was Honolulu where we took tours. Then on to Wake Island, on to Tokyo, Japan—here we saw many of the things Louise and I had seen on our Orient trip. Again to Hong Kong and the Philippines.

Bangkok was new to me and very interesting and I enjoyed the sights.

After Bangkok we sailed to Benares, India, Agra, Jaipur, Delhi. A short trip to Kashmir was enjoyable.

Nellie and her friend Annette Goheen
about to board a plane on their way to Kashmir.

In Beirut, we went over the great Arabian desert and our tour of this was overcoming.

After visiting Lebanon and Cypress, we arrived in Damascus and then through the Holy Land with all its Biblical history.

Then it was Cairo, Istanbul, Athens, Rome. After leaving Italy, it was beautiful Switzerland, and on to Paris, Brussels, Amsterdam, the Hague.

We arrived in London and no fog as we had three days of beautiful sunshine. A side trip to Shakespeare country. A wonderful 2 months and 25,000-mile trip was completed when we arrived home to good old USA.

28th

In 1954, I took another tour with the Campbells on an African Safari.

Nellie's photograph of Istanbul Harbor by the Galata Bridge.

Nellie wrote: "Native camp where we spent night on 5 day Safari Zululand. Rondavel huts for 2. Kraal for family. Image depicts a road with parked cars that splits a small village or camp in two. The small huts with round roofs are called rondavel. A kraal is a traditional African village of huts, usually surrounded by a fence."

This flight started from New York on the Sabena Airline,[45] a 12-hour flight and we landed in Brussels. From Brussels we flew to Cairo, on to Ethiopia, on to Nairobi, Mombassa, Zanzibar, Bagamoyo where saw the famous Victoria Falls,[46] and then to Johannesburg. There we saw the famous Kimberley mines where diamonds are mined.

We then went to South Africa, Port Elizabeth, The Transkei, Pondsland, Durban, Zululand, Swaziland, into the Belgian Congo, to Elizabethville, Lake Kivu, Albert National Park where we saw many of the African wildlife, pygmies, missions and native dances.

Soon after leaving this section, we were in Tunis, Carthage, Algiers, Morocco, Casa Blanca, Rabat, then on to Lisbon, Toledo, Madrid El Escorial.

We then flew to Paris and arrived there on Armistice Day and Paris was all aglow.

We departed for home after a short stop at Brussels to change planes, and quite a long stop in Iceland due to wheel trouble with our plane which made us a little late getting into New York but a wonderful 2 ½ months trip.

29th

In 1956, my brother Cyril wanted me to take another around-the-world trip with him, so I consented.

This was more-or-less a duplicate of the round-the-world trip I took in 1953, however, there was one variation for which I was glad: this tour included Australia and New Zealand. I had never seen those two places, and they were well worth seeing.

---

45. Belgian Limited Company for the Exploitation of Aerial Navigation was the national airline of Belgium from 1923 to 2001.
46. Victoria Falls is located between Zambia and Zimbabwe. Bagamoyo is a port city in Tanzania, nearly 1,500 miles distant.

30th

In 1968, Charlotte made arrangements with Goldie and Willard Lutz to take me up to the two ranches they had purchased in Merced and Colusa [California].

We left early in the morning and arrived in Merced in mid-afternoon and got a nice motel. Lewis, Chris and little Todd came down to the motel and had dinner with us. This was the first time I had seen my great-grandson Todd Mathis.

The next morning we went to Lewis' home and he took us all over this beautiful 21,000-acre ranch, an ideal ranch for cattle with a beautiful lake on it and rolling hills. In the evening, Chris had prepared a wonderful steak dinner for us.

The next morning, we wended our way to Calusa where Glenn had engaged a motel for us. Again this was my first time seeing my other great-grandson.

The next day "Deke" (Glenn) took us all over the Colusa ranch of 17,000-acres, another wonderful ranch for cattle, and we were

*Louise showing off her barn to her mother, Nellie,
on the ranch in Buellton, Calif.*

fortunate in seeing 3,700-head that had been rounded up for shipment the next day.

We left Colusa the next a.m. and stopped off at Oakland for one hour to see Goldie's brother, then on to Carmel for the night.[47]

On our return trip home we took the San Simeon highway on a clear, sunshiny day. This brought back many fond memories of years ago when I painted many of the beautiful scenes I had painted [along this route].

On our way down, we stopped at Buellton and found Mr. Evans who had sold part of the ranch Louise had just purchased and he took us around to show us this magnificent ranch of 7,000 acres.

We put up for the night at Santa Barbara. The next morning we drove back to my home after a very nice trip and I was so glad to

---

47. We do not know who "Goldie" refers to.

have seen all the ranches, my grandchildren and their wives, and my great-grandchildren.

31st

In 1969, Louise and Ivar took me to their ranch at Buellton, spending four days and seeing all of the ranch and the buildings, which I was unable to see last year as the gates were locked.

What a beautiful ranch in the interior, especially this year due to all the rains we had.

Louise has a very nice home on the ranch, which she has remodeled and painted, as well as several other homes for the help and a barn 300 ft long.

I enjoyed this trip immensely.

Nellie overlooking Louise's ranch in Buellton, 1969.

Endnotes—*Living Memories*

1. Laguna Woods & Leisure World

In 1960, real estate developer Ross W. Cortese, aided by research conducted by a self-funded gerontology program at the University of California, began construction on Leisure World Seal Beach, the first significant planned retirement community in the United States, welcoming its first inhabitants in June 1962. That same year, Cortese purchased 2,775 acres of the Moulton Ranch in south Orange County for about $6 million to begin development on his second 55-and-up community, known at the time as Leisure World Laguna Hills (Baker). According to Marjorie F. Jones, Laguna Woods' first

Historical Society archivist, in 1962 one could find Cortese "riding around the ranch property in the company of Mrs. Nellie Gail Moulton." Construction on the community began in 1963, with the first residents arriving on September 10, 1964. The land under Leisure World Laguna Hills remained unincorporated until 1999, when Laguna Woods was incorporated in Orange County (LW Community Information). Today, Leisure World, known as Laguna Woods Village, is a premiere 55-plus community featuring resort-style amenities for its residents and guests, including two professional golf courses, a 10-court tennis facility, an equestrian center, and more than 250 clubs and organizations (LW Community Information & Haldane). The name change resulted from a dispute between residents and the daughter of Cortese, Heidi, who filed a lawsuit to prevent the use of the Leisure World trademark on the community's website or cable TV advertising, asking for an annual $18,000 fee from residents to continue using the moniker (Haldane). Throughout Cortese's life, he oversaw the construction of seven Leisure World communities nationwide, including the Seal Beach and Laguna Woods locations (Baker).

References:

Baker, Terry, "The History of Leisure World 1963-1975," *The Historian*, July-August 2009.

Haldane, David, "Leisure World Getting Used to New Name," *Los Angeles Times*, Oct 11, 2005.

Laguna Woods Community Information, LagunaWoodsVillage.com.

2. Wizard of Oz

Author Lee Sandlin, in his book, *The Untold History of America's First Tornado Chasers*, theorized that Baum's central character Dorothy Gale may have been named after a victim by the same name who was found deceased face down in a mud puddle following the dual tornadoes (Pollak). However, historian Sally Roesch Wagner contends the famous protagonist is actually named after Baum's niece, Dorothy Louise Gage, who died in infancy likely due to either meningitis or equine encephalitis (Elleson, McLean). Baum released *The Wonderful World of Oz* in 1900 and would complete thirteen more novels in the series, with the last two being published shortly after the author's passing (Lyle).

References:

Pollak, Michael, "Where Twisters Dug In, So Did They," *The New York Times,* May 27, 2013.

Elleson, Lisa, "Gage, Dorothy Louise, June 11, 1898-Nov 15, 1989," McLean County Museum of History.

Lyle, "The Oz Books: Chicago History Classics," Chicago Public Library, April 24, 2016.

3. Irving, Kansas

Irving, Kansas, named after the esteemed 19th-century author Washington Irving, was founded in 1859 in the northeastern part of the state in Marshall County by colonists from Lyons, Iowa. The nascent midwestern community faced several challenges, including drought, bouts of intense inclement weather, and grasshopper "plagues" in 1866 and 1875. On May 30th, 1879, two tornadoes flattened much of the town, killing and injuring many. (Nellie recalled eighty-one as the number of deceased; modern reports put the number at nineteen.) Estimated property damage came in at nearly $65,000 (Fitzgerald, pp. 47–50), or roughly $2.1 million today (Westegg.com inflation calculator).

In 1952, the U.S. Corps of Engineers began construction on the Tuttle Creek reservoir, colloquially referred to by locals as "Big Dam Foolishness" (Fitzgerald, p. 42). As a result of the reservoir project, Irving and nine other northeastern towns located in the Big Blue River Valley became uninhabited ghost towns (U.S. Army Corps website). The area where Irving once stood has since become integrated into a wildlife refuge.

References:

Fitzgerald, Daniel, *Ghost Towns of Kansas: A Traveler's Guide,* University of Kansas Press, 1988

4. Kansas-Nebraska Act

In 1820, the Missouri Compromise was passed by Congress and signed into law by President James Monroe to "prohibit slavery in the Louisiana Purchase lands north of the 36°30' parallel." Later, in 1850, Senator Stephen Douglass pushed a bill known as the Compromise of 1850, which welcomed the territories of Utah and New Mexico into "the Union with or without slavery as their constitution may prescribe at the time of their admission." In 1854, to construct "a feasible transcontinental railroad" and increase settlement in the West, Douglas introduced the Nebraska Act, which would later colloquially become known as the Kansas-Nebraska Act. Douglas argued that the 1850 Compromise, which gave Utah and New Mexico the choice of whether or not to implement slavery, voided the Missouri Compromise of 1820, therefore opening up the possibility of slavery in Nebraska territory. The Kansas-Nebraska Act passed the Senate and the House and received authorization by President Franklin Pierce in May 1854. The Nebraska territory was thus split into two separate territories, Nebraska to the north, and Kansas to the south (Rawley, pp. 68–71).

The Kansas-Nebraska helped precipitate the Civil War, as it enabled these new territories to choose whether or not to allow slavery in lands where the Missouri Compromise had previously banned it. The Whig Party split into pro and con factions, dissolved, and former members created an abolitionist party known as the Republican Party. The first Republican president was Abraham Lincoln, a family friend of the Moultons.

References:

Rawley, James A, *Race and Politics, "Bleeding Kansas" and the Coming of the Civil War*, Lippincott, Philadelphia, 1969.

5. John Brown

John Brown believed that to hold a fellow human being in slavery was a sin against God. In 1847, Brown met Frederick Douglass, an escaped slave who published an essential "abolitionist newspaper called the North Star" and would become one of America's most important figures in the abolitionist movement. During this meeting, Brown expressed to Douglass his plan to usher enslaved people into the Allegheny Mountain Range and arm them in order to "destroy the money value of slavery property" (Dubois). Douglass came away from the meeting "less hopeful of [slavery's] peaceful abolition." With the Compromise of 1850 came the Fugitive Slave Act, a law that enforced the return of all runaway slaves to their owners. In defiance of the act, Brown formed the United States League of Gileadites, "an all-black resistance organization in Springfield" which "pledged to arm themselves, be ready to use their weapons at all times, and shoot to kill" (Sterngrass).

On October 16, 1859, Brown, his sons Watson, and Owen, and several anti-slavery compatriots began their raid on Harpers Ferry, a United States military arsenal "located where the Shenandoah and Potomac rivers merge." Brown attacked Harpers Ferry chiefly because it "was the safest natural entrance to the Great Black Way ... where there were massed in 1859 at least three of the four million slaves" (Dubois). By the next day at noon, hordes of volunteer militias composed of pro-slavery Southerners were firing upon Brown and his men and President James Buchanan had "ordered three artillery companies and 90 marines to Harpers Ferry." Two days later, "U.S. marines under the command of Colonel Robert. E. Lee broke into the engine room where Brown would be captured and much of his remaining cohort slain." John Brown was hanged at 11:15 a.m. December 2, 1859, with several faces of future Civil War notoriety in the crowd, including Thomas "Stonewall" Jackson, a Confederate General, and John Wilkes Booth, President Abraham Lincoln's assassin. After the events of Harper's Ferry, Douglass, reflecting on his friend, Brown, would write, "His zeal in the cause of freedom was infinitely superior to mine—it was the burning sun to my taper light. ... I could live for the slave; John Brown could die for him." (Sterngass)

References:

Du Bois, W.E. Burghardt, *John Brown*, George W. Jacobs & Company, Philadelphia, 1909.

Sterngrass, Jon, *John Brown*, Chelsea House Publishers, New York, 2009.

6. Native American Tribes of Kansas

Kansas was home to numerous Native American tribes during the 19th century; however, by the 1870s, increasing European encroachment in the area led to many tribes' forced removal from their ancestral lands and placement into reservations (Oklahoma Historical Society). The Native Americans Nellie Gail interacted with as a child could have belonged to any of the Arapaho, Cheyenne, Comanche, Jiwere, Kickapoo, Kiowa, Ochethi Sakowin, Ogaxpa, Osage, Pawnee, Peoria, Sauk and Meskwwaki, and Wichita tribes (Haswood). The state of Kansas itself was named after the "Kaw Nation," also known as the "Kanza" or "Kansa" people. The name *Kansas* translates as "south wind people" or "wind people" (U.S. Dept. of Interior). In 1873, the Kansa people, which only had 500 members at the time, were forced out of Kansas by the U.S. military to live on a reservation. As of 2011, there were 3,500 members of the Kansa Tribe (Tanner). Today, the state of Kansas is home to four federally recognized tribes, including the "Iowa Tribe of Kansas and Nebraska (White Cloud), the Kickapoo Tribe in Kansas (Horton), the Prairie Band Potawatomi Nation (Mayetta), and the Sac and Fox Nation of Missouri in Kansas and Nebraska (Reserve)" (Haswood).

References:

Tanner, Becky, "Native Americans: the first Kansans," *The Wichita Eagle*, Feb 20, 2011.

Haswood, Christina, "Native Americans in Kansas have a bright future," *Kansas Reflector*, Jan 21, 2021

"Origin of Names of US States," US Department of the Interior Indian Affairs, Jan 4, 1974.

7. Horace & Tribune

Founded in 1866, Horace, a city located in Greeley County, Kansas, was named after author Horace Greeley, the founder of the *New York Tribune* and the Liberal Republican nominee for president in 1872 (Gannett, p. 161). According to 2020 U.S. Census data, Horace is home to 102 people and 29 families. Other Kansas towns include nearby Tribune, likely named after Greeley's *New York Tribune*, and Greeley, which Nellie mentions in the Flight Journal. Horace Greeley uttered the legendary, "Go West young man, go West," when directing Josiah Bushnell Grinnell to report on the Illinois Agricultural State Fair (Grinnell, 86-87).

References:

Gannett, Henry, *The Origin of Certain Place Names in the United States*, Washington Government Printing Office, 1905.

Grinnell, Josiah Bushnell, *Reminiscences of Forty Years*, D. Lothrop Company, Boston, 1801.

8. Home Remedies

Castor Oil: Castor oil has been used "for thousands of years as a natural treatment for various health issues" (Healthline.com). Castor oil is a vegetable oil derived from a plant called *Ricinus communis*, which commonly grows in the global East. Today, in the United States, the Food and Drug Administration has only approved castor oil for its use as "a stimulative laxative for the temporary relief of occasional constipation." Off-label uses not approved by the FDA "include wound healing, arthritis, headache, menstrual cramps, and labor induction" (NIH).

Sulfur and Molasses: According to a *Time Magazine* article from 1946, "old wive's tales hold that sulfur and molasses ... provides a needed thickening of the blood, thinned down by Winter; the concoction is to be taken in early Spring" (Time Magazine, 1946). Blackstrap molasses, commonly used in this concoction, is the most concentrated form of molasses produced after three boiling sessions; it is thicker, darker, and more bitter-tasting than other kinds of molasses. In alternative medicine, sulfur and molasses are said to be used to maintain healthy blood sugar levels. Other potential benefits of the combination include preventing anemia, lessening the likelihood of developing osteoporosis, and aiding digestion (Juber, 2022).

Mustard Plaster: Mustard plaster is created using an equal mixture "of flour and powdered mustard," it should then be applied to a piece of cloth and spread as a paste. Although it should be treated as a folk medicine, many still use mustard plasters to treat rheumatism, arthritis, chest congestion, aching back, and sore muscles (Yabanoglu, 2012). According to healthline.com, there is no verifiable data to prove the benefits of mustard plaster, and adverse side effects such as skin irritation and burns could result from its application to the skin. Other safer alternatives to treat similar ailments include decongestant nasal sprays, over-the-counter nonsteroidal anti-inflammatory drugs, and cough and cold medications.

Eucalyptus Oil: Eucalyptus oil is derived from the leaves and branch tops of the eucalyptus tree. The leaves contain flavonoids, natural plant-based antioxidants, and tannins, which some researchers say, "may help reduce inflammation." Eucalyptus is used to treat the common cold and can be found in many modern medicines, including lozenges, cough syrups, rubs, and more. Eucalyptus oil has also been found to help in the treatment of arthritis, boils, sores, and wounds (Mount Sinai).

References:

Alookaran, Jeffrey; Tripp, Jayson, "Castor Oil," National Center of Biotechnology Information, May 24, 2024.

"4 Benefits and Uses of Castor Oil," Healthline.

"Medicine: Spring Fever," *Time*, March 25, 1946.

Juber, Mahammad, MD, "Blackstrap Molasses: Are There Health Benefits?" WebMD.

"Does Mustard Plaster Work for Coughs and Colds," Healthline.

Akbulut, Sami; Karakayali, Feza; Yabanoglu, Hakan, "Phytocontact Dermatitis due to Mustard Seed Mimicking Burn Injury," PubMed.

"Eucalyptus," Mount Sinai.org.

9. Pastor Moody

Dwight L. Moody, 1837–1899, one of America's most consequential evangelists, converted to God in a shoe store in Boston, Massachusetts, in April 1855 after his Sunday school teacher, Edward Kimball, visited him and told the young man "of Christ's love for him, and the love Christ wanted in return." At the age of 19, Moody moved to Chicago and opened a Sunday school in the city's slums; in November 1860, President-elect Abraham Lincoln visited the school, giving an impromptu Sunday school address to the students. During the Civil War, Moody, who "held deeply to the cause of the Union" and whose "New England origins had fostered strong abolitionist views" visited the front nine times to conduct relief work.

From June 1873 to July 1875, Moody went on his first gospel mission to Great Britain, a watershed event for the evangelist. An essay published in the *Oxford Dictionary of National Biography* described Moody and his ministerial partner and composer Ira Sankey's impact as representing "the chief cultural influence of the United States on Britain during the nineteenth century." As a result of their two-year-long mission, thousands were converted, and thousands of nominal Christians were led into closer communion with God. At the outset of the trip, Moody used practically all the financial capital he had, approximately $100, to print a sixteen-page pamphlet of hymns written by Sankey. The book of hymns, eventually picked up by a British publisher, garnered no less than $35,000, or $750,000 in modern currency.

In November 1899, Moody set out on a gospel tour of the American West. He delivered his final sermon, titled "Why Not Be a Christian" with text from Luke 14:18 at the Great Hall in Kansas City in front of 15,000 people. After becoming ill and bedridden, he died in December of 1899 in the place of his birth, Northfield Massachusetts. Upon learning of Moody's passing, President McKinley wrote a letter to the preacher's family in which he wrote, "The effect of Mr. Moody's great services to mankind will long endure as a fitting monument to his noble character and purposes."

References:

Belmonte, Kevin, *D.L. Moody–A Life: Innovator, Evangelist, World Changer*, Moody Publishers, Aug, 2024.

10. Jay Gould

During his lifetime, there were few businessmen so reviled by the public and the media as Jason (Jay) Gould, a Wall Street trader who went on to become one of the United States' leading railroad tycoons. While Gould's fortunes had many ups and downs according to business historian Julius Grodinksy, by 1881, Gould was in control of approximately 15,854 miles of railroad, or 15% of the national total.

In his *New York World* newspaper, Joseph Pulitzer lambasted Gould as "one of the most sinister figures that have ever flitted bat-like across the vision of the American people." Many who knew Gould personally felt differently, with Ezra Cornell, a board member on Gould's Western Union rail, calling his boss "the most misunderstood businessman in the country [and] one of the most remarkable men America has produced." Unlike several of his robber baron peers, Gould avoided Gilded Age debauchery, stayed loyal to his family, and enjoyed horticulture and reading from his personal library (Klein, pp. 166-172).

References:

Klein, Mary; Calandro, Joseph Jr., "Jay Gould, the Union Pacific Railroad, and Value Creation," Museum of American Finance, Fall 2016.

11. Chicago World's Fair

The 1893 Chicago World's Fair, also known as the Columbian Exposition, celebrated the 400th anniversary of Christopher Columbus's coming to America. Architect Frederick Law Olmsted and partner Henry Codman dredged a system of canals from Lake Michigan through 600 acres of Jackson Park and Midway Plaisance to build the grounds. Temporary by design, the fair became known as the White City because of the color scheme of its primary buildings built of plaster, cement and hemp, a composite lighter than wood.

Each state building had the unique heritage and character of the individual state in mind. California was represented in the style of an old Spanish mission, Virginia by a replica of Mount Vernon, Illinois' pavilion resembling the state's capital building (Bolotin, p. 32–34). Several foreign nations, including France, Great Britain, and Spain, constructed buildings in their national architectural traditions on the lakefront. Sophia Hayden of Boston won a competition to design The Woman's Building, "a graceful Italian Renaissance structure."

The most popular attraction, designed by George Washington Ferris, was the "Ferris Wheel," which carried forty people (Nellie Gail among them) in each of its thirty-six railcar-size cabins.

References:

Bolotin, Norm, *The World's Columbian Exposition: the Chicago Worlds Fair of 1893*, University of Illinois Press, 2002.

12. El Toro & El Toro Store

In 1846, Don Jose Serrano acquired Rancho Serrano through a Mexican land grant (Fox). Native American ranch helpers began to refer to the place as El Toro due to the herds of cattle headed by "bellowing bulls." However, not until 1888, when the Santa Fe Railroad began operating in the area, would all residents start referring to the town as El Toro (Moulton).

There is no exact date for when the original El Toro general store opened its doors, but we know that the first station agent of El Toro, O.D. Fairchild, built the two-story building which served as a "store, post office, and hotel." Later, James Delong, a section foreman on the local railroad, bought the building and leased it to several tenants. The first was Charles Lyon, followed by three others in the 1890s, including "David Gockley, Bob Squires, and James Lucas" (Fox, p. 41). Following Lucas's tenure, Nellie Gail's father, John Lockwood Gail, became the storekeeper in 1901 and received help from Nellie's sister Carrie Gail. Two years later, John and Carrie departed for Moneta, California, where John became the postmaster (Fox, p. 55). The final head of the original store was Mr. A. A. Avery, whose initials led to the store being called "the Three A Store" or the "Triple A Grocery" (Whitcomb).

In either 1917 or 1921, a fire burned down the original El Toro general store while Delong still owned it; there is historical disagreement on which year the fire occurred, and no one knows how it started. Locals had to make their way to Irvine or San Juan Capistrano by train or horse and buggy to purchase groceries and other home goods (Whitcomb).

In 1921, brothers Bennie and George Osterman opened a new general store close to where the original had burned. The final owner of the Osterman building was a Basque man with an extended family ranching history in South County named Noelie M. Changala, who ran the store from 1966 until its permanent closure in 1976 (OC Historyland).

References:

Fox, Clara Mason, *A History of El Toro*, 1937, El Toro Women's Club.

Moulton, Charlotte, "El Toro and Its History," *Orange County History Series, Volume 2*, 1932.

Whitcomb, Janet, "What Ever Happened to El Toro's First General Store," Sept 29, 2012, Patch.com.

"El Toro Post Office," OCHistoryland.com.

13. Ben-Hur

The famous play for which Lewis Moulton managed to procure tickets for himself and Nellie Gail was based on the novel *Ben-Hur: A Tale of the Christ* published in 1880 by Civil War General Lew Wallace (Swansburg, 2013). The novel, play, and film adaptations follow the life of Jesus and a fictional Jewish prince, "Judah Ben-Hur, who suffers betrayal, injustice, and brutality and longs for a Jewish king to vanquish Rome" (Lifson, 2009). Presidents Ulysses S. Grant and James A. Garfield both praised the novel, with Garfield saying, "With this beautiful and reverent book, you have lightened the burden of my daily life" (Swansburg, 2013). President Garfield even gave the author the position of minister plenipotentiary to the Ottoman Empire.

Between 1880 and 1912, one million copies of the novel were sold; in 1913, "Sears Roebuck ordered a million more, at the time the largest book order ever placed" (Swansburg, 2013). In 1899, Wallace agreed to a *Ben-Hur* stage production, which became a Broadway sensation. In 1925, Fred Niblo directed the silent film, and its 1959 remake garnered 11 Oscars, including Best Actor for Charlton Heston.

References:

Swansburg, John, "The Passion of Lew Wallace," *Slate*, March 26, 2013.

Lifson, Amy, "Ben-Hur: The Book that Shook the World," *Humanities,* Nov/Dec 2009, Volume 30, Number 6.

14. James Irvine Sr. & family

James Irvine Sr. was born in Anabilt, County Down, Ireland, on December 27, 1827, and lived happily with his eight siblings and parents on a farm until Ireland's potato famine wiped out over a million Irish. In 1846, Irvine and his younger brother William joined in the great departure, leaving from Belfast, arriving the same year in New York, and later, in 1848, journeying to California to partake in the gold rush (Irvine Ranch History, p. 17). In the early 1850s,

Irvine joined other family members to raise sheep. In 1864, during a great drought, Irvine and family purchased the 48,803-acre Rancho San Joaquin from Don Jose Andres Sepulveda for $18,000 (Irvine Ranch History pp. 9, 18).

In 1874, James Irvine Sr employed 20-year-old Lewis Moulton as a shepherd.

During another drought in 1876, Irvine made the wild decision to buy out his partners for $150,000, becoming the sole owner (Irvine Ranch History, p. 23). According to historian Jim Sleeper, Irvine died in 1886 due to complications from Bright's disease, leaving his estate, worth $1.2 million, to his wife Margaret and his 18-year-old son James Harvey Irvine Sr. "who was to inherit the remainder of the estate when he reached the age of 25" (Irvine Ranch History, p. 27).

Many years later, in 1960, under the direction of architect William Pereira, the Irvine Company produced the Irvine Master Plan, laying out the foundation for thousands of homes and businesses (Berg, 2018). Incorporated into Orange County in 1971, the 2020 census counted 307,670 residents.

References:

"The Irvine Ranch History, From Mexican Land Grant to Great Irvine Ranch," Irvine Historical Society.

"Irvine Development to 1950s," Irvine Historical Society.

Berg, Tom, "How Irvine Became America's Best Planned City," *Irvine Standard*, Sept 26, 2018.

15. Kaspare Cohn

Born in Loebau, Prussia, in 1839, Kaspare Cohn emigrated to the United States in 1859 at 20 years old upon receiving an invitation from his uncle, Harris Newmark, to work for him at his grocery store in Los Angeles. During his tenure working at Newmark's grocery store, Cohn was instructed by his uncle to sleep on the floor of the store to dissuade burglars from stealing the $40,000 to $50,000 kept in the store's safe by Los Angeles County Treasurer Maurice Kremer, Newmark's cousin, on account of there being no banks in Los Angeles at the time.

After a short-lived stint in Red Bluff, California, where Cohn opened a crockery shop, the failed retailer returned to Los Angeles, where he joined his brother Samuel and Newmark in a wholesale venture that "purchased wools and hides from local ranchers." Lewis Moulton and Cohn's friendship likely began as an ordinary business partnership, as Cohn was tasked with the wool side of the business.

Eventually, shepherds who were often away from home began storing their money in Cohn's personal safe, with Cohn holding as much as $300,000 in shepherds' funds at a time. With Cohn's safe overflowing, California law required that he form a banking corporation. In 1914, Cohn, along with his sons-in-laws Ben Meyer and Milton Getz, founded Kaspare Cohn Commercial and Savings Bank, which would become Union Bank after Cohn died in 1916.

Cohn founded Kaspare Cohn Hospital in 1902, initially located in a modified two-story building in Los Angeles, which has today become the distinguished Cedars-Sinai Medical Center (Harrison, 2024).

Several letters between Lewis Moulton and his brother Irving (an employee of Union Bank) show that Cohn acted as a liaison between the brothers while Irving lived in San Francisco.

References:

Harrison, Donald H., "Kaspare Cohn's Legacies: Union Bank, Cedars-Sinai Hospital," *San Diego Jewish* World, January 21, 2024.

16. Madame Helena Modjeska

Madame Helena Modjeska, born on October 12, 1840, in Krakow, Poland, was one of ten children and was raised mainly by her great-aunt Teresa while her mother worked (Modjeska, p. 15). The stage actress played many notable Shakespearean roles, including Ophelia, Juliet, Desdemona, and Queen Anne in *Richard III*. In 1876, Modjeska, her second husband Charles Bozenta Chlapowski, known to friends as "The Count," and Polish writer Henryk Sienkiewicz, along with a few others, decided to take a trip to America in Modjeska's words, "to get away from Warsaw and the unfriendly spirits as soon as possible" (Modjeska, p. 247). Eventually, the plan to get away turned into a plan of emigration and Chlapowski envisioned establishing a colony on a farm in California (Modjeska, p. 249). While living on a small farm and cottage, Modjeska became acquainted with and made friends with Joseph Edward and Maria Refugio Pleasants (Pasco).

On a return visit to California in 1883, upon the invitation of the Pleasants, Modjeska and her husband ventured out to the Pleasants's home in the Santiago Canyon, taking a "three-hour horse-and-buggy ride from the El Toro train station" to get there. In 1888, Modjeska and Chlapowski bought the 1,340-acre ranch and Pleasants' home (Pasco, 2005). Modjeska called the property "Arden" after the forest of Arden from Shakespeare's *As You Like It* (Modjeska, p. 294). Modjeska and her husband tasked the much-lauded architect Stanford White to carry out the design and construction of what would become known as the Modjeska House around the cottage that had been inhabited by the Pleasants (Modjeska, p. 540–541). White would go on to design some of the most important American structures in history, including Madison Square Garden, The Washington Memorial Arch, and the New York Herald Building (nps.gov).

The area in south Orange County known as Modjeska Canyon, just north of Trabuco Canyon, was so named shortly after the passing of Madame Modjeska in 1909. Modjeska's historic home and gardens can be visited during docent-guided tours provided by OC Parks.

References:

Modjeska, Helena, *Memories and impressions of Helena Modjeska; an autobiography*, The Macmillan Company, New York, 1910.

Pasco, Jean O., "Modjeska House a Retreat for All," *Los Angeles Times*, Feb. 28, 2005.

"Stanfard White," National Park Service.

17. Judge Egan of Capistrano

Richard Egan was born in County Waterford, Ireland, in 1842, and at ten years of age, came to the United States where he would be educated on the East Coast. The Irish youth fought alongside the Confederate Army as a blockade runner during the American Civil War and later sailed around Cape Horn to San Francisco in 1866. Egan, one of Lewis Moulton's closest friends, was San Juan Capistrano's *alcalde*, a term used by the Spanish to denote someone who simultaneously held the titles of "mayor, judge, and chief dignitary." In 1870, Egan was elected as the city's Justice of the Peace and became the city's first telegraph operator; Egan took great pleasure in impressing guests with his extraordinary aptitude for multitasking (SJC Historical Society). Another friend of Moulton's, the famous Polish stage actress Madame Helena Modjeska, dubbed Egan "The Capistrano King" (Whitcomb, 2014). The King was a bona fide polyglot, proficiently speaking five languages, including "French, Italian, Polish, Spanish, and English" (SJC Historical Society). Egan's home still stands in downtown San Juan Capistrano. Residents and visitors can stop by Ellie's Table, a quaint cafe inside of Egan's original red-brick home, and enjoy an assortment of breakfast fare, pastries, and coffee.

References:

Whitcomb, Janet, "Remembering Judge Egan, The King of Capistrano," *Orange County Register,* Dec. 27, 2024.

"Judge Richard Egan – 'The King of Capistrano,'" San Juan Capistrano Historical Society, April 13, 2021.

18. Helen Hunt Jackson

In 1879, forty-nine-year-old Helen Hunt Jackson attended a speech delivered by Ponca Indian Chief Standing Bear in Boston and decided to make Native American rights her *cause célèbre.* Jackson wrote *A Tale of Dishonor: A Sketch of the United States Government's Dealings With Some of the Indian Tribes* in 1881 and distributed it to all members of Congress. Inspired in part by her friend Harriet Beecher Stowe's *Uncle Tom's Cabin*, Jackson aimed to publish a novel that would expose Americans to the plight of Native Americans in an accessible way. She locked herself away in a New York City apartment to write for three months and published *Ramona* in 1884 (Niemann, 2022). The novel follows the lives of Ramona and her husband Alessandro, the son of a Luiseño chief at Mission San Luis Rey, and the constant prejudices the couple deal with, culminating in the murder of Alessandro. Although *Ramona* was a smashing success, her hopes of the novel spreading social change to enact better treatment of the nation's native population did not materialize (Komanecky, 2020). Jackson passed away due to complications caused by cancer less than a year after the publication.

References:

Niemann, Greg, "CV History: Helen Hunt Jackson, Advocate for American Indians and Author of *Ramona*, Proved One Person Can Make a Difference," *Coachella Valley Independent*, July 10, 2022.

Komanecky, Michael, "Behind the Scenes: The Story Behind *Ramona*," Farnsworth Art Museum, April 28, 2020.

19. Jean Pierre Daguerre & family

Jean Pierre Daguerre was born in May 1856 in Hasparren, Basses-Pyrenees, in the mountainous Basque region between France and Spain. Daguerre traveled from France "to the United States in 1874 at 18 and began work as a shepherd at the Rosecranz Ranch for the family of Domingo Amestoy." Daguerre and his wife Maria Eugenia Duguet had four children, starting with their son Domingo, followed by daughters Juanita, Grace, and Josephine (Letter, pp. 2–3). In 1895, after working for a time as a ranch manager for Lewis Moulton, the two would eventually come to an agreement, founding the Moulton Company, which gave Daguerre a one-third holding of the ranch, which at the time spanned approximately 19,500 acres (Fox, p. 48). Most of Daguerre's land holdings were located where modern-day Laguna Niguel sits (Moulton

Museum Website). In 1911, at the modern intersection of Crown Valley Parkway and Cabot Road, Daguerre's horses were spooked by an automobile, launching him off his wagon headfirst into the ground where he "suffered massive head injuries and died" (Letter, pp. 6–7). Daguerre left his youngest daughter, Josephine, responsible for taking "care of the business, being the competent secretary of the company for some years" (Fox, p. 49). In 1912, Moulton and Domingo Daguerre, Jean Pierre's son, decided to sell their sheep and restock the ranch with cattle (Letter, p. 7). Domingo died during the influenza epidemic of 1919 (Fox, p. 49). The partnership between the Moulton and Daguerre families dissolved at the outset of the 1950s, resulting in the selling off of the families' land for modern development (Letter, p. 9).

References:

Letter, Barbara, "Moulton Ranch and The Jean Pierre Daguerre Family," Laguna Woods History.org, 2018.

Fox, Clara Mason, *A History of El Toro*, 1937, El Toro Women's Club.

"J.P. Daguerre," Moulton Museum, June 29, 2022.

20. Laguna Niguel

According to the city of Laguna Niguel's official website, the city was named after the Spanish word *Laguna*, which means Lagoon, and the Juaneño Native American village called "Niguelí" which was once located near Aliso Creek. A resident of San Juan Capistrano, Juan Avila acquired the land that Laguna Niguel sits on today through a Mexican grant in 1842, eight years before California became a U.S. state. Avila owned Rancho Niguel until he sold it to Cyrus Rawson in 1865. In 1895, Moulton purchased Rancho Niguel from Rawson and founded L.F. Moulton & Company (Moulton Museum website). The real estate firm Cabot, Cabot, and Forbes created the Laguna Niguel Corporation and assembled the first drafts in 1959 for one of the first master-planned communities in the United States. In 1989, Laguna Niguel became the twenty-ninth city to be incorporated into Orange County, California, after 89% of residents voted in favor of incorporation.

References:

"History," CityofLagunaNiguel.com.

"History of Laguna Niguel," LagunaNiguel.com.

"Meet Lewis Fenno Moulton," MoultonMuseum.org.

21. Ebell Club in Los Angeles

Dr. Adrian John Ebell was born on the island of Ceylon in Sri Lanka in 1840 and moved to New York at the age of ten with his elder sister. The young Ebell graduated from Yale in 1866 and later graduated with an M.D. in 1869 from Albany Medical College (Beckelheimer). During a tour to California in 1876, Ebell, along with 20 women at Oakland's chapel of the First Congregational Church, founded "The Ebell Society for the Advancement of Women," the first of many Ebell women's clubs (Rathman).

The Ebell Club of Los Angeles, to which Nellie Gail and her friend Ozzie Ogen belonged, was modeled after the original club in Oakland. On a Saturday morning, October 27, 1894, Misses Emmie and Alice Parsons held "the meeting for the organization of the Ebell" of Los Angeles at their residence, 1026 South Olive St. From 1905 to 1927, the club met at The Figueroa Club House located at 1719 South Figueroa St., likely where Gail and Ogen attended. In 1926, architect Sumner Hunt drew up the plans for an elaborate complex of club rooms and a 1,300-seat auditorium in the Italian Renaissance style: the Wilshire Ebell Theater (Ebell Club of LA). The editor of this volume, Scott T. Barnes, received a Writers of the Future Award in that same venue eighty-five years later for his short story, "Insect Sculptor."

References:

Beckelheimer, Alberta, "Adrian John Ebell, M.D.," The Ebell Club of Anaheim.

Rathman, Mrs. Charles F. (Harriet E. Bigelow), *The Ebell of Los Angeles, 1894-1952.*

EbellofLA.org archives.

22. Annette Galbraith Goheen

Annette's granddaughter sent the Moulton Museum this lovely note: "Annette Galbraith Goheen was a friend of Nellie Moulton's. I do not know when their friendship began, but I believe it was when they were children. My grandmother was born in Hebron, Nebraska, in 1880. She later moved to Evanston, Illinois, and died there in 1977. Throughout their lives, my grandmother visited Nellie in California, and they also traveled together. I know that one trip was to Hawaii. My grandmother went to Europe in the 1920s, but I don't know if Nellie went on that trip. (*Yes, see Flight Journal 19~STB.*)

"My grandmother had seven of Nellie's paintings. I have six, and my brother has one. Of the paintings I have, one is of beautiful decaying arches from a long-ago structure with vines hanging from it. Another is of trees near a lake; the others are of ocean waves and rocks. Five of them are signed. My brother's painting is of a cabin or barn with a windmill. I'm updating my will and designating that Nellie's paintings are to stay with my partner if I die first. Upon her/our death(s), they are to be given to the . Thank you, Roberta Majka."

23. World's Fair NYC

Nellie Gail and her youngest daughter Louise could not have attended the 1939–1940 World's Fair in Chicago because that particular World's Fair, which celebrated the 150th anniversary of George Washington's inauguration, was held in New York City. Another city hosted a World's Fair from 1939–1940, yet it too was not held in Chicago but on Treasure Island in the San Francisco Bay. It is possible that Nellie Gail mistook the year and the pair attended the 1933 World's Fair in Chicago, also known as the "Century of Progress," a celebration of Chicago's 100th birthday and "progress in science and industry over the past 100 years." However, it is most likely that they attended the New York City World's Fair in 1939 due to its proximity to Boston, where the two traveled from.

References:

Roesch, Roberta, *World's Fairs, Yesterday, Today, Tomorrow*, The John Day Company, New York, 1967.

24. Emperor Haile Selassie/Rastafarianism

The origins of the religion and philosophy of Rastafarianism lie in the prophecy issued by Marcus Mosiah Garvey, a Jamaican born in August 1887. Garvey, a black nationalist, founded the Universal Negro Improvement Association (UNIA) and believed all people of African origin "should return to their rightful homeland, Africa." Garvey prophesized, "look to Africa, when a Black king shall be crowned, for the day of deliverance is at hand." Ten years later, in 1930, Garvey's message seemed to manifest itself in the crowning of Ras Tafari Makonnen in Ethiopia. Makonnen, whom Nellie Gail visited on her trip to Africa in 1954, took the name Haile Selassie upon assuming his role as emperor (Martin). Leonard P. Howell, a top-ranking associate in Garvey's inner circle, returned to his native Jamaica after spending time in the United States and appointed himself Selassie's representative in Jamaica. Howell, sometimes referred to as "the first rasta," believed that Selassie was the great Black Messiah. He preached the divinity of the Ethiopian emperor and penned the first book on Rastafarianism, *The Promised Key: The Sublime Essence of Rastafari* (Williams).

While Selassie accumulated thousands of Rastafarian followers who believed him to be a living God or "Jah," Selassie never accepted deification (Kerkhof). During an interview in 1967 with Canada's CBC, Selassie told Rastafarians, "clearly that I am a man, that I am mortal, and that I will be replaced by the oncoming generation, and that they should never make a mistake in assuming or pretending that a human being is emanated from a deity."

In 1974, Selassie was deposed by a Marxist-Leninist military junta called the DERG. This led to Colonel Mengistu Haile Mariam's rise to power and his "Red Terror," which murdered tens of thousands. Following Selassie's death, many Rastafarians came to see Selassie not as a deity but as a symbol of African resistance, empowerment, and a key figure in the struggle against oppression (Kerkhof).

References:

Martin, Tony, "Marcus Garvey," BBC, Oct 21, 2009.

Kerkhof, Maup van de, "Why Do the Rastafari Believe That Haile Selassi Was a God?" *The Collector,* May 1, 2024.

Williams, Paul H., "Black History: Leonard Howell the first Rasta," *The Gleaner,* Feb 2, 2014.

25. Song Titles

"Over There" by George M. Cohan, 1917.

"Ka-Ka-Ka Katy" by Geoffrey O'Hara, sung by Fred Field, 1918.

"Pack up Your Troubles in Your Old Kit Bag" by George and Felix Powell, 1915.

"Keep Home Fires Burning While Hearts are Yearning," Lyrics by Lena Guilbert Ford: Composed by Ivor Novello, 1914.

"How Can You Keep Them Down on the Farm After They've Seen Paree'," Lyrics by Joe Young and Sam M. Lewis, composed by Walter Donaldson, 1919.

"Only a Bird in a Gilded Cage," Lyrics by Arthur J. Lamb, composed by Harry von Tilzer, 1900.

"After the Ball" by Charles K. Harris, 1891.

"A Hot Time in the Old Town Tonight" by Theodore August Metz, 1896.

"When You Were Sweet Sixteen" composed and written by James Thornton, 1898.

Acknowledgements

Most images in this publication are drawn from the holdings of the Moulton Museum. Several others are attributed to their respective institutions in the captions. We also acknowledge photographic research help from the Anderson Historical Society, Kansas University, Port Orchard Historical Society, the Pioneer Museum, and California Historical Society.

Many people contributed to the successful completion of this project. In no particular order, the following people deserve special thanks:

Jane Barnes–carrying on the family legacy and sharing stories of Nellie Gail

Jeff Ashley–researching and drafting the endnotes

Jean Stearn–reading the original manuscript and providing such a thoughtful introduction

Barbara Markey–copy editing an early draft

Elisabeth Lange–extensive help with researching and editing, and in particular for finding photos and writing captions

Jennifer Keil, Cindy Keil and 70 Degrees–discovering Nellie's long-lost memoir and starting the process of seeing it published

Jacquelyn Sharga–social media and promotional assistance

Allyson Longueira–interior design and layout

Eric Stoner–high resolution photos of the Gail and Stoneman families

The Book Break–cover design, Kickstarter campaign, and promotion

The Moulton Family for making this all possible and especially Jared Mathis for reviewing manuscript versions and championing the project.

All the Kickstarter contributors, listed and unlisted, you have our thanks, and especially our sponsors Tim Smith Real Estate Group and Farmers & Merchants Bank.

The volunteers of the Moulton Museum who tirelessly share the story of Nellie Gail and Lewis Moulton.

Kickstarter Sponsors

Tim Smith of Tim Smith Real Estate Group
Warren Paez of Farmers and Merchants Bank
Franklin Barnes
Tony Terreri
Tina Alfaro
Ellen Thomas
Sandy Wheeler
Laguna Woods History Center
Bonny Briney
Stephanie Hibbits
Dave Hutton
David Wolf
Kevin Akash of Tiller House
Craig Holly
Joanna Laznicka
Wendy Brunt
Claudia Di Napoli and Family

About the Editor

The editor of *Living Memories, A Memoir* is also Nellie Gail Moulton's great-grandson. Scott T. Barnes has published oral histories, a fourth-grade reader, and works of young adult fiction, including the novel *Memories of Lucinda Eco,* which *BookLife* called "a spellbinding blend of magic and mystery." Scott's science fiction story "Insect Sculptor" won the *L. Ron Hubbard presents Writers of the Future Award.* More about Scott's work can be found at www.scotttbarnes.com.

If you enjoyed *Living Memories* you may also enjoy
these other works by editor Scott T. Barnes

Two oral histories from
the gold mining town of Julian, California

A true-life fourth-grade reader set on
the desert Rancho San Felipe, east of Temecula, California

See all of Scott's work at http://www.scotttbarnes.com

MOULTON™ MUSEUM

Moulton Museum is proud to uphold the pioneering spirit of Lewis and Nellie Gail Moulton. We preserve documents related to early Orange County history and California's ranching legacy. *Living Memories* is our first publication, and an important contribution to local history.

We invite anyone interested in learning more about Nellie Gail or Orange County to visit us at the Moulton Museum, located in the Moulton Ranch Center, Laguna Hills.

Opened in 2022, the Moulton Museum features a 2500-square-foot historical exhibition and a 1000-square-foot fine art gallery, both of which are open to the public free of charge. Moulton Museum is a space where people can come together, learn, and appreciate the legacy of South Orange County and its notable figures.

VOLUNTEER OPPORTUNITIES

EVENT AMBASSADOR   CLASSROOM EDUCATOR

GRANT WRITER   RESEARCHER   DOCENT

to join, visit moultonmuseum.org

 www.moultonmuseum.org

 info@moultonmuseum.org

 25256 Cabot Rd. Laguna Hills CA 92653

 (949) 8-MUSEUM